BLOOMSBURY VISUAL ARTS
Bloomsbury Publishing Plc, 50 Bedford Square, London, WC1B 3DP, UK
Bloomsbury Publishing Inc, 1359 Broadway, New York, NY 10018, USA
Bloomsbury Publishing Ireland, 29 Earlsfort Terrace, Dublin 2, D02 AY28, Ireland

BLOOMSBURY, BLOOMSBURY VISUAL ARTS and the Diana
logo are trademarks of Bloomsbury Publishing Plc

First published in Great Britain 2020
Reprinted 2025 (twice)

Copyright © Anitra Nottingham and Jeremy Stout, 2020
Anitra Nottingham and Jeremy Stout have asserted their
rights under the Copyright, Designs and Patents Act, 1988,
to be identified as Authors of this work.

Cover and Interior design: Jeremy Stout and
Anitra Nottingham

All rights reserved. No part of this publication may be: i) reproduced or transmitted in
any form, electronic or mechanical, including photocopying, recording or by means of
any information storage or retrieval system without prior permission in writing from
the publishers; or ii) used or reproduced in any way for the training, development or
operation of artificial intelligence (AI) technologies, including generative AI technologies.
The rights holders expressly reserve this publication from the text and data mining
exception as per Article 4(3) of the Digital Single Market Directive (EU) 2019/790.

Bloomsbury Publishing Plc does not have any control over, or responsibility for, any third-
party websites referred to or in this book. All internet addresses given in this book were
correct at the time of going to press. The author and publisher regret any inconvenience
caused if addresses have changed or sites have ceased to exist, but can accept no
responsibility for any such changes.

A catalogue record for this book is available from the
British Library.

Library of Congress Cataloging-in-Publication Data
Names: Nottingham, Anitra, author. Stout, Jeremy, author.
Title: The graphic design process: how to be successful in
design school / Anitra Nottingham and Jeremy Stout.
Description: London ; New York, NY: Bloomsbury Visual Arts,
2020   . | Includes bibliographical references and index.
Identifiers: LCCN 2018047361| ISBN 9781350050785
(pbk. : alk. paper) | ISBN 9781350050792 (epdf) | ISBN
9781350050808 (ebk)
Subjects: LCSH: Commercial art—Study and teaching.
| Graphic arts—Study and teaching.
Classification: LCC NC1000 .N68 2019 | DDC 740.71—dc23
LC record available at https://lccn.loc.gov/2018047361

PB: 978-1-3500-5078-5
ePDF: 978-1-3500-5079-2
ebook: 978-1-3500-5080-8

Printed and bound in Great Britain

For product safety related questions contact
productsafety@bloomsbury.com.

To find out more about our authors and books visit
www.bloomsbury.com and sign up for our newsletters.

BLOOMSBURY VISUAL ARTS
LONDON • NEW YORK • OXFORD • NEW DELHI • SYDNEY

To find out more about our authors and books visit www.bloomsbury.com and sign up for our newsletters.

Online resources to accompany this book are available at: www.bloomsbury.com/the-graphic-design-process-9781350050785

Please type the URL into your web browser and follow the instructions to access the Companion Website. If you experience any problems, please contact Bloomsbury at: companion-websites@bloomsbury.com

Introduction 06
The purpose of this book 06
How graphic design school works 10

PART 1
ABOUT THE DESIGN PROCESS

Design thinking 14
Thinking like a designer 15
Learning to be creative 17
The trouble with 'design thinking' in graphic design 19
The design process is sometimes messy 20

The 4D design process 23
Discover 23
Design 24
Develop 25
Deploy 26

How this book is structured 27
How to search this book 27
What is your teacher looking for? 28

PART 2
USING A DESIGN PROCESS

Chapter 1: Discover 30
Kicking off a design project 32
The design brief 36
Understanding the design problem 46
Case studies 55
    A tight brief 55
    An explorative brief 58
    A blended brief 61
    A loose brief 64

Chapter 2: Design 68
Divergent thinking 69
Techniques for generating ideas 78
Design exploration using sketches and drafts 92
Case studies 99
    Divergent thinking 99
    Loose sketches 103
    Tight sketches 108

Chapter 3: Develop 112
Convergent thinking 112
Working with your instructor 122
Working with the critique 127
Case studies 133
    Asking questions 133
    Subjectivity 136
    Critique 139
    Group critique 143

Chapter 4: Deploy 146
Presenting your work 148
Design juries, panels, committees and clients 160
Understanding your grade 165
Case studies 171
    Professional style presentation 171
    Using a narrative 175
    A slide presentation 179
    Online presentation 181

Glossary of key terms 184
Annotated further reading 190
Index 194
Acknowledgements 199

INTRODUCTION

THE PURPOSE OF THIS BOOK

Success in graphic design comes from knowing the intricacies and best practices of the profession. The same applies to design school. The more you understand about how things work in your design education, the better your chances of success. Our goal in this book is to give you tips, perspectives and methods for understanding the best practices typically found in graphic design schools around the world.

Design studio classes are a unique learning experience, and the way classes, projects and feedback work are different to the schooling most students have previously experienced. Therefore, many new design students have issues understanding exactly how to approach their

Design teacher and student in a classroom together.

teachers and their projects. Often, students do not know why teachers say what they say or do what they do, so design learning can sometimes be confusing for students. This can make the graphic design school experience seem daunting, and even discouraging, at the start.

This book explains how to navigate the creative process in the context of graphic design studio classes; from receiving a brief, to successfully presenting your final project. We do this by breaking the creative process down into phases, giving you practical information about design decisions, teacher critique, and expectations, along the way.

We have written extensively about each of the design phases and how to practically apply their theoretical aspects to your work. We have included explanations and examples of design school assignments for each phase. *These examples include analysis and critique by design teachers from a range of different graphic design schools.* Our goal is to help answer a common design student questions: What is my teacher actually looking for and how do I do it?

CONTRIBUTING —— UNIVERSITIES AND COLLEGES

Parsons School of Design,
New York, USA

CalArts,
Los Angeles, USA

Otis,
New York, USA

University of California at Los Angeles,
Los Angeles, USA

University of Illinois,
Champaign County, USA

California College of Arts,
San Francisco, USA

North Carolina State University,
Raleigh, USA

University of Nevada,
Reno, USA

Plymouth College of Art,
Plymouth, United Kingdom

Monash University Design School,
Melbourne, Australia

University of Maryland,
College Park, USA

Ferris State,
Grand Rapids, USA

Academy of Art University,
San Francisco, CA

How do we know what your design teachers[1] are looking for? We are two long-time graphic designers and teachers, as well as former design school students ourselves. We see (and experience) the challenges of design school first-hand every day, and have helped many students through their graphic design degree and on to career success. We have studied how the graphic design studio works, spoken with teachers, and gathered material from design schools around the world.

We know that a good understanding of how the creative process works and a clear idea of what is expected of you as a student is key to your success. We designed this book to provide advice on a range of topics such as:

- Understanding a design brief
- Coming up with ideas
- Making good decisions
- Generating and presenting ideas
- Producing the final project

Along the way, we also talk about the differences between school and the professional world, in order to help you step from school into your first design job.

Like everything in the world, graphic design school has a context. Each design school has a different set of circumstances that form the setting and the way it can be understood. At the same time there are some shared expectations and processes within the design studio — or 'rules' of the classroom — that they all share. What this book is not intended to do is replace your design teacher or prescribe how every design studio or

---

[1] We struggled with what to call your design instructor, because the term changes depending on where you are. In Australia where Anitra lives, and in the UK where our editor is located, the term 'tutor' is common, and 'teacher' is sometimes used. In the USA where Jeremy lives the terms 'instructor' or 'professor' are most often used. Some online schools use unfamiliar terms such as 'learning facilitator'. We ended up with the term 'teacher' as it seems to best sum up the role no matter where you are.

This book is a guide you can pack for your journey through design school.

project 'should' proceed. Every design teacher and graphic design school is different: with its own culture and approach to being creative. The wonderful thing about design teachers is that they all have different ways of approaching design and you can learn something from all of them. This book helps to explain design teacher feedback, instruction, and guidance but not to dictate how they should teach. Instead, you can *think of this book as a guide to the creative process and how to survive and thrive in design school, and beyond.*

Now that you know what this book is generally about it is time to look briefly at how design education works.

HOW GRAPHIC DESIGN SCHOOL WORKS

Most students enter school with little or no knowledge of how the design studio classroom works. So, at first, the classroom can seem baffling, and might even sometimes feel unfair. Understanding a bit more about how a design studio class works, right from the beginning, will make what happens there more understandable and the expectations more achievable. Let's start from the basics.

The design studio class (*design studio,* or *just studio*) is named after the designer's professional workspace. Many professional studios are set up in open spaces, so designers can see and talk to each other, with large tables that can hold computers and printed work, and with walls that work can be pinned up on. Design studio classrooms usually look similar to these professional spaces.

Students working at the Academy of Art University in San Francisco.

A professional designer's studio.

The design studio classroom has ways of working that are similar to a professional studio. Students and teachers work together to develop design projects that can run anywhere from a few days to a few semesters! Work is completed in, and outside of, class time. During class, teachers talk about the student work. Teachers will usually encourage (or require) students to talk about each other's work as well, which makes the classroom interactive. This is quite unlike a university lecture hall where students tend to sit and listen to their teachers with little interaction between them.

Teachers in design studio classrooms do 'lecture' by explaining design principles, showing examples and giving demonstrations, but this is usually informal, and doesn't take up the whole class session. Mostly teachers talk to students about how to improve their work, and this talk is called 'critique', (or 'crit'). Critique is when you get vital feedback that you are expected to use to improve your projects. Critique is the heart of design teaching and learning: We learn design by doing, and by talking about the work as it unfolds. In class you will spend the majority of your time having your work critiqued, speaking about other students' work and seeing the teacher's critique of other student work.

There are many different ways teachers critique. In group critique the teacher will talk about each student's individual project in front of all of the students. This form of critique is especially helpful if all of the students are working on the same project brief. It allows everyone to see the feedback of fellow students and apply that critique to their own work. Another way teachers critique is to 'cruise' or 'patrol' the classroom talking to students in a 'one-on-one' (sometimes called a 'desk crit') and working side-by-side at the computer, and/or 'marking up' printouts by drawing and writing on them. Critique modes change based on what you are working on and what is the best way for you to learn, as well as the classroom space and the type of project. There is a good chance you will experience many other different types of critique during design school.

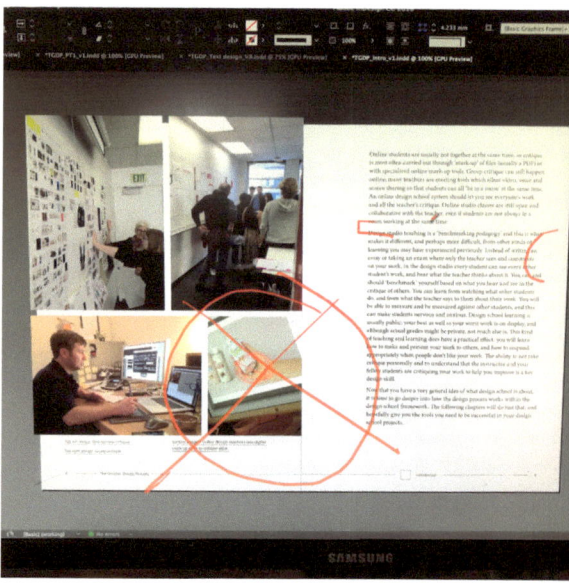

Top left image: One-on-one critique.

Top right image: Group critique.

Bottom images: Online design teachers use digital mark-up tools to critique work.

The Graphic Design Process

Online students are usually not together at the same time, so critique is most often carried out through 'mark-up' of files (usually a PDF) or with specialised online mark-up tools. Group critique can still happen online; many teachers use meeting tools that allow video, voice and screen sharing so that students can all 'be in a room' at the same time. An online design school system should let you see everyone's work and all the teacher's critique. Online studio classes are still open and collaborative with the teacher, even if students are not always in a room working at the same time.

Design studio teaching is a 'benchmarking pedagogy' and this is what makes it different, and perhaps more difficult, from other kinds of learning you may have experienced previously. Instead of writing an essay or taking an exam where only the teacher sees and comments on your work, in the design studio every student can see every other student's work, and hear what the teacher thinks about it. You can and should 'benchmark' yourself based on what you hear and see in the critique of others. You can learn from watching what other students do, and from what the teacher says to them about their work. You will be able to measure and be measured against other students, and this can make students nervous and anxious. Design school learning is usually public; your best as well as your worst work is on display, and although actual grades might be private, not much else is. This kind of teaching and learning does have a practical effect: you will learn how to make and present your work to others, and how to respond appropriately when people don't like your work. The ability to not take critique personally and to understand that the instructor and your fellow students are critiquing your work to help you improve is a key design skill.

Now that you have a very general idea of what design school is about, it is time to go deeper into how the design process works within the design school framework. The following chapters will do just that, and hopefully give you the tools you need to be successful in your design school projects.

Part One

ABOUT THE DESIGN PROCESS

DESIGN

THINKING

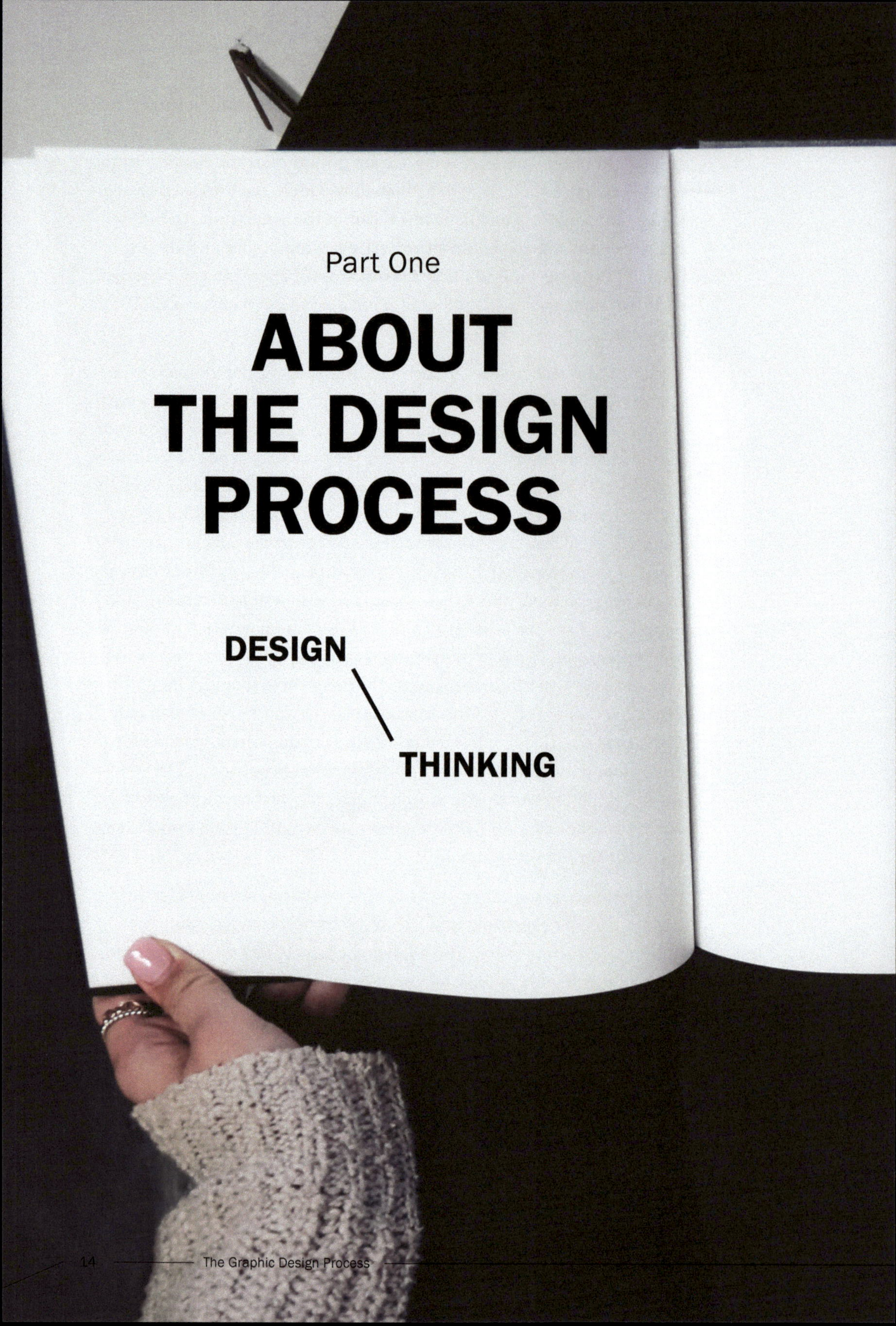

Being a graphic designer means that you need to be 'creative on demand', generating visual and conceptual ideas consistently and to schedule. In both school and practice, you will need to generate ideas and good design, even when you feel tired, overworked or uninspired. To do so you will need to develop a design process that fosters and supports creative thinking. An effective design process that you can rely on to help you focus, and to open paths to your creativity, is one of the major things you are learning in design school. Part One of this book explains how most design processes share common ideas and methods. We begin by explaining the way designers think and how they learn to be creative, and why a design process is necessary to success. We finish with an explanation of the '4Ds': a framework for the design process that helps us to produce creative projects. In Part Two we explain how the 4D framework can be employed in your own graphic design projects in school and beyond.

THINKING LIKE A DESIGNER

The term 'design thinking' is often used to describe the way designers in any discipline (product, service, fashion, industrial, etc.) work through a design problem. 'Design thinking' breaks the designer's process down into a series of steps as follows:

Design process steps >>

1. *Define the problem:* This usually involves some sort of research.

2. *Create many different ideas and options:* This is called 'divergent thinking'.

3. *Refine the best ideas:* This is called 'convergent thinking'.

4. *Steps 2 and 3 may be repeated.*

5. *Pick the best idea:* Make prototypes and sometimes test them on users (user-testing) to refine the final design.

6. *Steps 2, 3 and 4 may be repeated* until the final design solution is completed.

Design thinking has been visualised and presented as a creative process, much like in the diagram below. You will find many kinds of designers, including graphic designers, saying they use a 'design thinking

Opposite page: An open sketchbook, a designer's most essential tool.

 About The Design Process

1	2	3	4	5
Discovery	Interpretation	Ideation	Experimentation	Evolution
Understand the challenge Prepare research gather inspiration	Tell stories and search for meaning, frame opportunities	Generate ideas and refine ideas	Make prototypes and get feedback	Track learnings Move forward

Number of Possibilities

The design-thinking process ocellates between divergent and convergent modes

This diagram is based on the IDEO's visualisation of the design thinking process. Many point to IDEO as the origin of design-thinking in graphic design. Certainly through their books, talks, tools and online courses, IDEO are the most visible proponent of design thinking as a creative process method.

process', or 'design thinking methodology'. If you hear this, it means that a designer solves problems by generating lots of ideas, refining and user-testing, before choosing and producing a final.

'Design thinking' is currently accepted as a process applicable to solving all kinds of problems, but it is a contested idea in the graphic design community because it somewhat glosses over exactly how to do the 'creative' part of the design process. Some doubt that a series of steps adequately explains the way graphic designers work – so we will explore this idea further in a moment. However, the simplicity of design thinking does demystify the design process and makes it easier to understand the way we learn to design, so it's a good place to start.

LEARNING TO BE CREATIVE

Designers have to be creative to do their job. There are two ways of thinking about being creative. The first, and most commonly held idea is that there is something unique about designers: that they are just 'creative people' born with a special talent that design school nurtures. The other idea is represented by 'design thinking': design is not a unique ability, rather it is a process and a tool, which can be learned and used by designers and non-designers alike.

Some design theorists[1] have broken down the design process into a series of 'easily repeatable' steps, which implies the creativity of the individual designer is not important. As long as you follow the steps, design will result. Other theorists[2] have argued that designers have special abilities, something they call a 'designer's intuition' or a 'design eye', which means that the designer as a person is essential to the design process. In this view, without the designer's creative abilities there can be no design.

We agree with both views. Designing is a series of steps that can be learned, but it is the way a designer applies their intuition to the steps that makes the 'magic' happen. However, intuition isn't a natural inborn talent that some possess, and others do not. A designer's intuition is also a series of steps that can be learned. A design idea does not come into our minds like a lightning bolt of inspiration, even if it sometimes feels that way. An idea is the result of a series of small thinking 'leaps' or 'creative connections', which design theorist Nigel Cross calls a creative bridge. Designers mentally 'walk' across the creative bridge to an idea, rather than making a big mental leap across nothing to an idea. Designers often cross the bridge in a subconscious way, and this is why it looks like 'talent'. Some people are naturally 'more creative'

---

1 Such as Dan Norman and Herbert Simon, see further reading, p. 190
2 Including Nigel Cross, Donald Schön, Bryce Lawson and Patrick Buchanan, see further reading, p. 190

because they can more easily make creative connections before they start training. This is why we say that graphic design is not a 'mysterious, ineffable art'[3] that only a talented few can master. A designer's intuition is just a special way of thinking that must be learned and honed through practise. The most compelling evidence that we may be right is of course that all sorts of people learn to be graphic designers all the time. Some people just more effortlessly walk over the creative bridge without much practise, while others might have to crawl across it, at least at first. As is so often the case though, the harder you work, the more 'talented' you become.

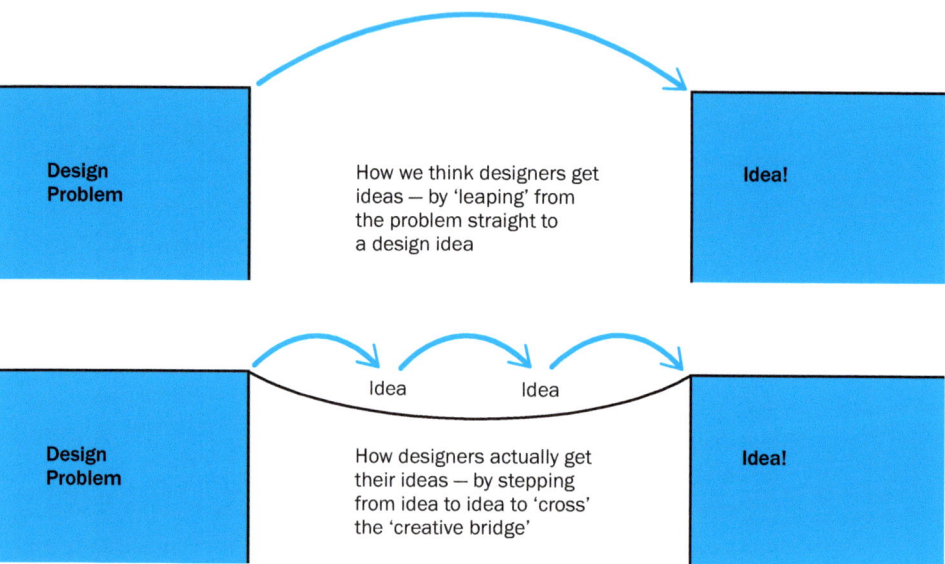

The Creative Bridge as described by Nigel Cross.

---

3 Nigel Cross in *Designerly ways of knowing* (1999, p.7).

THE TROUBLE WITH 'DESIGN THINKING' IN GRAPHIC DESIGN

When broadly applied to the graphic design process, 'design thinking' might look as follows:

<u>Design thinking steps</u>
>>

1. *Define the problem:* A project brief is given to, created (or modified) by the designer, who may conduct and/or be supplied with research to help them understand the problem.

2. *Create many different ideas and options:* The designer generates multiple rough initial ideas and drafts.

3. *Refine the best ideas:* The designer creates multiple iterations and prototypes of a number of ideas to find the best one.

4. *Steps 2 and 3 may be repeated.*

5. *Pick the best idea and produce:* Craft and produce the work to the required specifications. The designer may or may not test the final design on users.

It must be noted however, there is no prescribed or exact way of working that all graphic designers follow – only generally held and commonly shared ideas. Although this process broadly applies, not all graphic designers follow the steps in the order we presented here. Other visualisations of the graphic design process have five or seven steps rather than four, and the steps can often overlap or be repeated. All graphic design teachers teach a design process[4] of some kind.

While design thinking maps to the general graphic design process we outline here, it has been criticised for several practical reasons. While some graphic design projects benefit from extensive research and user testing, others do not. Testing on audiences has a patchy track record in predicting success. Some designers argue that user research stifles innovation because the audience is not an expert in good design,[5] and usability is not always the only concern in graphic design.

Most criticism of design thinking surrounds its focus on process over aesthetics: It is possible for a designer to follow the design thinking

---

4   They may call it a creative process.

5   Henry Ford was not entirely wrong when he said if he had asked the audience what they wanted they would have said a faster horse rather than a car.

process steps exactly, all the while making poor visual and conceptual decisions, and end up with a bad design. This point is important because aesthetics matter in graphic design. As Pentagram Designer, Natasha Jen, notes: 'Beauty is precision and intelligenc – not decoration, aesthetics is essential to the success of a design, not an optional add-on.'

Effective graphic design must catch the audience's attention and then compel them to keep looking so that they take in the message and (hopefully) take the desired action. It is often aesthetics that allow designers to make this happen. You could call graphic designers 'affect engineers' in that they engineer designs to make the audience feel something. Feeling cannot be easily engineered because it is often a response to how something looks (aesthetics), not always to how it works (usability). Although graphic designers care about usability (for example, typography needs to be readable when used in a book), it is not always the primary consideration. Graphic designers are in some ways akin to fashion designers as they constantly seek out graphic forms that the audience haven't seen before – and don't even know that they will like yet.[6]

Apart from a concern about aesthetics, some teachers shy away from the design-thinking process because it assumes design is always a series of repeatable steps. Repeatable steps make the creative process seem easy, or at least smooth, and sometimes this just isn't true.

THE DESIGN PROCESS IS SOMETIMES MESSY

The word 'process' implies something linear: leading from uncertainty to certainty, from rough to refined. In reality the design process is often erratic. Some ideas seem to spring fully formed into our minds, while others require many (sometimes painful) rounds of sketches and drafts. Sometimes designers get stuck – the equivalent of 'writer's block' – which makes the designer unable to create new ideas, circle around the same ideas, or even go backwards.

---

[6] Which is perhaps why user-testing is not that predictable in graphic design. Like a new fashion trend, people may need time to become familiar with a style before they will like it.

Blindly following the design-thinking steps isn't a reliable recipe for good design outcomes as we have noted; following steps puts the focus on process often to the detriment of outcomes. The designer's intuition must be applied to the decisions made during the design thinking process for it to be a success. Intuition is a feeling, so it isn't certain. Meaning we can't always be confident about our design choices, and that self-doubt can lead to getting stuck or backtracking during the design process. Additionally, a designer's intuition is a particular way of thinking that can be developed, but it doesn't come naturally to everyone. This means that the design process will take some people longer to learn. Some students will achieve higher levels of design skill based on their ability to build their design eye.

All this is to say that you should expect, and learn to be patient with, a certain amount of messiness and uncertainty in the design process. We'll talk more about this uncertainty and when to be concerned about

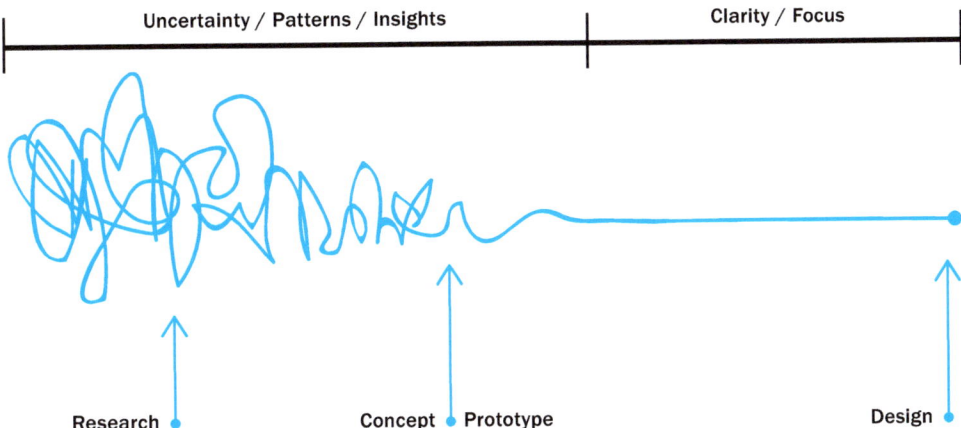

This is one of the best infographics of the many you will find to describe the design process; it acknowledges that the best kind of process can be messy but ultimately productive. We have taken this idea from designer Damien Newman.

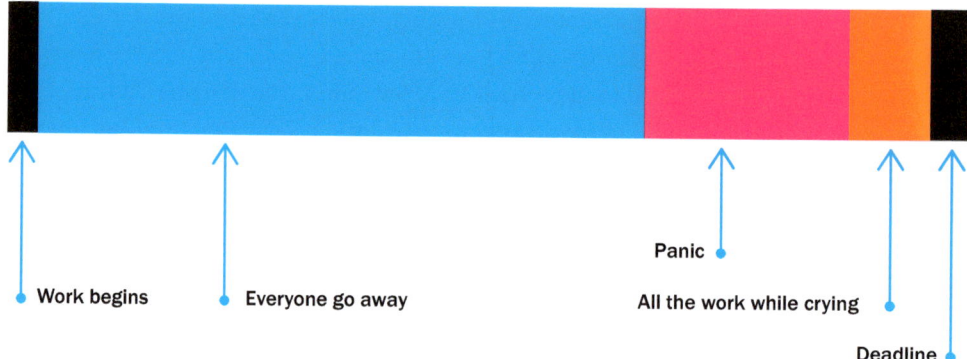

This is what tends to happen without a design process. We have taken this idea from an original (and somewhat profane) cartoon by Drew Fairweather.

getting stuck and backtracking later in the book. For now, let's just say a design process does not always move easily forward in a logical fashion, and that's ok. Using a process is much, much better than not using one; having a process to follow helps organise, focus and channel our creativity. Design school is a great space to learn and cultivate your unique design process. Once you master using any design process end-to-end you can then modify, ignore and generally customise the steps to make a design process that works for you.

THE 4D DESIGN PROCESS

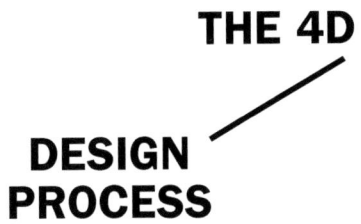

All creative processes are valid, including the design-thinking steps, if they help us reach a solution. All creative processes can be mapped to a framework called the '4Ds'. The 4Ds are so-called because the framework consists of four parts, each beginning with a 'D' as follows: 'Discover', 'Design', 'Develop' and 'Deploy'. Each 'D' is a stage, part, or phase of the creative process, and each phase overlaps, bleeds and leads into each other. The 4D framework is universal, in that it applies across many creative disciplines. You can describe the process of making a movie, carving a piece of sculpture, architecting a building, and designing a piece of graphic design using the 4D framework. We structured this book around the 4Ds because it does not lock you or your teacher into any one method, process or way of designing. Any project, creative process or method your teacher uses will map to the 4D process. What the 4D framework does is break down and isolate each of the steps common to all graphic design process so that you can successfully work through a project methodically from beginning to end.

Let's examine each of the four 'D's.

DISCOVER

In the 'discover' phase of the 4D process the goal is to research and gather information that leads to understanding the project, the topic and to gain insights[7] in order to generate ideas. Here, designers aim to learn as much about the topic and the design problem as possible, using a wide variety of multiple sources – both written and visual.

---

[7] An insight is not a fact. Having an insight means you have drawn information ideas, research and facts from various sources that your creativity and intellect has connected to form a new perspective, meaning or a new connection. A true insight is capable of generating new design ideas.

A good discovery phase will remain open and explorative; it asks you to look under every rock and turn over every stone, follow lines of inquiry, leads and references, and to ask questions.

At any point in the design process you might find new insights that will help develop your ideas. You may revisit the discovery phase during a project if you need additional insights or deeper understanding. Strive to end the discovery phase of the design process with as close to an expert understanding of the subject matter as possible. We sometimes say that if you could have a five-minute conversation about your topic with an expert and sound like you know what you are talking about, then you have a pretty good understanding. If you would look like a fool conversing with an expert for five minutes, you need to do more research. This level of understanding will create more effective designs that are based on facts and insights, rather than on misconceptions, personal likes or dislikes.

A design brief is the foundation and beginning of the project and provides an understanding of the project goals stated in clear terms. In a design school setting, the brief usually comes without, or with very little information compared to a professional brief, which is robust and detailed. A student brief can range from very tight and prescribed, to loose and explorative. In design school, getting the brief should be followed by conducting research to understand the topic, project and gain insights. You'll learn about different kinds of briefs and practical ways of going about the discovery phase in Chapter 3. The Discover phase, sets you up to begin the next phase of the process: 'Design'.

DESIGN

The goal of the 'Design' phase of the process is to generate conceptual and formal ideas. Divergent thinking is key: you must strive for multiple solutions tied directly to the research and results of the Discover phase. The research and brief created during the Discover phase is like a building block to erect your design upon. You gained understanding and knowledge and insights around the design problem, then stated the goals and outcomes in the brief. Now, during the design phase, you are looking for all the possible ideas – both visual and conceptual – that can answer the Design problem. There are many techniques used for generating conceptual and formal ideas that will be discussed later in the book.

Many people describe this phase of the design process as the most fun and creative. It is important to remember that during this stage, the designer must be open to failure as well as success. Following ideas, combining ideas and generating ideas can lead to success, but it can also fail – and this is ok. It is better to find out what does not work at the design phase; it will be much harder to find out later, having invested a lot of time and energy, that your ideas and resulting work are not, after all, usable.

Divergent ideas come about by investigating multiple formal and conceptual perspectives. Get out into the world and explore and work on thinking without preconceived judgement. If you kill an idea before it has a chance to grow, it is gone. The quest to generate ideas is important (and fun). Follow where ideas go so they can grow and blossom, then see where they went, evaluate them and rework them again.

The outcome of the design phase is usually sketches/rough computer drafts and ideas. A good set of ideas will have the potential to solve the design problem. If you exit this phase with lots of good ideas connected to your brief, you're on the right track. We'll talk more about ways to be creative in this phase in Chapter 4. At the end of the Design phase you should be ready to take your ideas to the next phase of the 4D process: 'Develop'.

DEVELOP

The 'Develop' phase of the design process is about decisions, refinement, and trial and error, often called 'convergent thinking'. You want to be making good formal, production, aesthetic and conceptual decisions. In this phase, things are removed and development is much more focused than it was in the Design stage. There is still room for exploration, user-testing and research, but the goal is to lessen the number of variables and to define a single strong design direction.

In design school your teacher will be quite involved in this phase. Early on, teachers usually act like creative directors, helping you to decide which of your ideas is the strongest and eliminating ideas that are not as promising. However, as you advance, the teacher usually acts more like your colleague, talking you through making these decisions yourself. It is important to develop the skill of creating multiple ideas and then choosing the ones with the most promise on your own. By allowing you to struggle through decisions, teachers are giving you the opportunity to learn about what makes a good or bad decision.

We will talk more about working with your teacher through this phase in Chapter 5. At the end of the Develop phase, you should have worked out the direction and details of your design. This will make you ready for the final phase: 'Deploy'.

DEPLOY

Here, in the final phase of the design process, you will put the work out into the world in finished form. Some projects may continue past this phase, requiring feedback about audience interaction to gauge effectiveness. For the purposes of this book, we will consider deployment the end of the process.

Deployment involves production of physical or digital comps and final art. Details and production are extremely important here. Spellchecking, image quality, making sure every link is live, checking every pixel, and leaving nothing to chance is key. Deployment can mean printing brochures and posters, or going live with an app or website. Sometimes this phase can mean putting your work into an exhibition, or submitting it for judging.

This phase often involves giving a presentation to the client. In design school, the Deploy phases usually involves giving a class presentation. The way that you present your work is paramount; talking about your work using the correct design terms helps to connect the presentation audience to your ideas.

A good visual presentation often means creating a narrative that communicates your ideas. You will be asked to decide how the different parts of your project fit together and describe how you solved the problem. These skills will be explained in greater depth in Part Two, Chapter 4.

HOW THIS BOOK IS STRUCTURED

This book is structured around the 4D design process and you can use it in multiple ways:

Ways to use this book
>>

1. *You can read this book from cover to cover* to get a complete idea of how the graphic design process works. We start from the initial brief and travel all the way through to the final presentation – the same order you would see a typical design school project unfold.

2. *You can choose to refer* to whichever phase of the process, or case study, you are most interested in. The book breaks up the information into the phases of the design process, and into specific case studies that illustrate these phases using real design school projects and teacher comments.

3. *The book can be used as a quick reference* for specific topics you want to know more about, such as writing a brief or making a presentation, etc.

HOW TO SEARCH THIS BOOK

Part Two of this book is exclusively devoted to using the four phases of the design process. Each chapter is titled with the name of one of these phases: Discover, Design, Develop and Deploy. Within each of these chapters the different aspects of the particular phase is broken down and explained in detail. At the end of each of these four chapters, we've used case studies to show examples of student work. These examples illustrate teacher expectations and will help you understand how to succeed while you are in design school. To help you transition to the working world, we illustrate where design teacher expectations are similar to, and differ from, client expectations.

Throughout this book this image will appear at the start of the case study sections.

WHAT IS YOUR TEACHER LOOKING FOR?

As we have said before; every design project – and design school – is different. It is impossible for us to be able to tell you exactly what it is your actual teacher is looking for. But we can show you – through case studies — what your teacher is looking for in terms of process: how much work, what kind of work and what kind of thinking they want to see as you work through a design problem.

In the Discover chapter (pages 30-67), we'll look at different kinds of brief. Teacher explanations will focus on the rationale for each brief and explain how teachers expect students to approach this initial phase of the design project. In the Design chapter, the examples illustrate instances of divergent thinking, and show students using different creative techniques, such as mind mapping, key words and mood boards. The teacher assessments here describe the strengths and weaknesses of the process work, showing what teachers think works best at this crucial phase of a design project. The Develop chapter contains examples of convergent thinking and the idea of problem spaces and solutions in action. Here, the teachers describe the strengths and weaknesses of the examples. This part includes an exemplar teacher critique to help you know what to look for (and what to ask for) from your teachers. In the final section,

Deploy, the instructor explanations will focus on what is expected from a successful design project presentation, so you will know how to give your projects that extra polish that helps 'sell' the work.

Designers are, on the whole, visual people who like to look at examples, so we will use examples in the book to bring to life some of the ideas we talk about in the text. All of the examples can be found on the website [insert URL here]. We have drawn this material from different kinds of design schools, from different levels of students, and from all sorts of design teachers using various instruction methods from around the world. The wealth of information we provide should help you succeed in whatever type of design school you attend.

We have written this book using accessible language to keep the ideas and concepts easy to follow. We understand that readers who are new to design do not have a complete understanding of the terms and phrases that are used by their teachers and in the professional world. The glossary at the back of the book helps to explain the graphic design and education terminology. Knowing the right terms allows you to better understand what your teacher is saying and to follow their instruction. When you learn the right terms to explain your formal and conceptual ideas to others, it makes you a better communicator and a stronger designer.

The design process is a wide and varied topic, and there is no possibility of covering every possible variation of this subject in one book. However, we do cover the introductory questions that you as a student might need answered in a straightforward and accessible way. We want to set you up to successfully navigate the world of graphic design school.

Part Two

USING A DESIGN PROCESS

CHAPTER ONE ——————

————— **DISCOVER**

Gather lots of information to help you understand the design problem.

A design project begins with discovery, where the goal is to research and gather information that leads to understanding and insights about the design problem. In a way, designers are like journalists; we must get our heads around complex information gathered by researching, asking questions and following lines of enquiry. Then we must distil and present this information in a way that viewers can easily understand – the difference is that designers present this information visually rather than just with words. We cannot present information to others if we do not understand it ourselves. Learn to ask good questions and be unafraid of asking what may seem like 'stupid' ones in order to help you understand a problem. Asking questions and analysing the answers is an important, but often unrecognised, design skill.

Opposite page: Open sketchbook and pen ready for design ideas.

 Discover > Design > Develop > Deploy

KICKING OFF A DESIGN PROJECT

In the professional world the Discover phase often ends with the production of a brief, but in design school discovery always starts with a brief. The brief is an integral part of the creative process in design school, so this chapter focuses on the different kinds of design school briefs and what you should do with a brief once you get it.

What is a brief?

A professional creative brief (or just a 'brief') is a document that outlines what the client would like a designer to deliver for payment. The brief will usually spell out the objectives and goals by stating what the project is, why it's being done, and the intended audience. The brief might also detail the specifications of formats, as well as the budget and the materials the designer has to work with. It might form the basis of a contract. There is no accepted standard for what is in a professional brief, just a host of best practices.

A design school assignment is modelled on, and named, after a professional brief. What is in a design school brief depends on the school, teacher, subject and level, so it can vary quite widely, as you will see in the case studies at the end of this chapter. Although there is wide variation, here are some items typically found in a design school brief:

Description: what the assignment is about

Objective/goal: what needs to be achieved with the design

Purpose: what skills/concepts are to be learned

Specifications and formats: what exactly must be created for the assignment

Tools/materials: what tools will be needed, and what materials are available/should be used for the assignment

Due dates: a school brief usually breaks a project down into stages with a final due date

School brief item list <<

Many school projects are run in much the same way as professional graphic design projects. There is a brief, a design problem must be understood (visual and other research), ideas will be worked through to produce a solution (sketches and drafts), refining until the best one is found and produced. Not all projects run this way and there are some crucial differences between a professional project and a school project.

The first difference is time. Student designers usually get a lot more time on a project so each step of the graphic design process is elongated, with more time for thinking, sketching, production and learning. While you are a student you are still learning how to design so it takes you longer than a professional to complete the same tasks. Another difference is budget, a consideration that rarely gets talked about in the classroom yet is one of the most important constraints on a professional project design.

What is a briefing?

In an on-site class the brief may be in the form of a printed handout. Online, the brief is usually integrated into the class materials. In addition to the brief, design teachers will often begin by presenting and discussing what you 'need to know' to be successful. Teachers want to give you pertinent information, answer questions and present any useful information in what is called a 'briefing'. In a briefing, your teacher explains (or 'briefs') you by speaking to and explaining the assignment. Briefing is often accompanied by lectures and demonstrations of skills relevant to the tasks in the assignment.

An important part of a briefing is the question-and-answer session, so be prepared to ask questions for clarification. Although online classes try to anticipate your questions in the class materials, be prepared to ask questions there too. It is crucial that you understand what is required of you so that you have the best chance of succeeding. Your goal at the end of a briefing session is to fully understand the problem you are tasked with solving, when things are due and to understand how far you can push the limits of the brief.

Visual examples in the briefing

Teachers often use visual examples during a briefing. These may be professional design examples and/or previous student work, which is called an 'exemplar'. Design is difficult to explain in words so examples and exemplars help you see what your teacher is saying and to describe what to do (or not to do) with the project. If your teacher doesn't use visual examples, ask if they have some.

Teacher shows exemplar work to student.

Exemplar work makes success more tangible. Teachers often use stories of past student successes or struggles, which can be a helpful way to understand where the difficult points of a project are and how you can overcome them. In the professional world, clients will rarely show you visual examples. It is a good idea to ask for, and to have, visual examples on hand to help clients talk about their project.

Many design school hallways are filled with exemplar student work to both inspire, and to remind students of the competition (other students).

THE DESIGN BRIEF

In a professional setting the client may supply the designer with a brief, or the designer will write the brief in consultation with the client. This means that in your career you will likely be called upon at some point to write a brief.

What is in a brief and how to write one

As we will discuss later, school briefs vary from 'loose' to 'tight', depending on how much student input is expected. This means you will be called on to partly formulate, and occasionally even to write your own brief for a design school project. To help you do this, here is a breakdown of each item usually found in a professional brief:

Company/topic description: Short description of the topic or organisation, its background and any market(s) it operates within; this gives the designer some of the context for the project.

Professional brief Items <<

Scope/specifications: What exactly needs to be created, including the size, format, media, functionality, page numbers, colours, etc. so that the designer can understand the full parameters of the project. Sometimes there might be some flexibility here, but often specifications are based on budget and so must be adhered to.

Objective/goal: What does this design need to achieve? Why? Without understanding the goal of the project it's not possible to know what the designer should aim for, or how to measure success. This one sentence can be surprisingly difficult to write as is requires distilling the very essence of the project in a short succinct statement.

Target audience(s): The brief needs to detail the intended audiences as well as defining which are the most important, or primary audience(s) and any other, or secondary, audience(s) so that the designer knows who the project is intended to reach. This is one of the most important pieces of information for the designer.

Budget and schedule: Important delivery dates are usually included, but clients will often decide not to give an exact budget at the beginning and provide only a ballpark spend, leaving room for negotiation.

Background: The history of the context the project is working within so the designer can understand what has and has not been successful, as well as what is fresh and what is stale within that context.

Brand: If the project draws upon a current brand or sub-brand there will be a description of the brand strategy, brand personality and any visual elements of the brand. (A set of branding guidelines may also be handed over for the designer for visual reference.)

Name: Some projects require the designers to come up with a name. If so, the specifics of what the name needs to do are included. If the project is already named an explanation of how the name was arrived at is useful as it can help to generate ideas.

Direct and indirect competitors: This information helps the designer understand who and what is competing with the project for wallet share and/or mind share. The design might need to avoid looking like the competition or, conversely, might need to look similar to the competition – whatever meets the objective best.

Unique Selling Proposition (or Point) – USP: A defining quality of the design that sets the subject of the project apart from the competition. This helps the designer to differentiate the project from its competition.

Single-Minded Proposition: What's the most important thing the audience needs to know about the project? This helps to focus and guide design decisions, helping the designer to discard ideas that are not central to the objective.

Product details: Sometimes the product is the company (for example, a branding project); if not then usually a design brief involves some kind of product (digital or physical). The product details might include things like price range and technical/functional specifications.

Reason the product/service is needed: What gap, or market opportunity is the product/service fulfilling? This will help the designer understand why the audience may be interested in the project and to generate ideas.

Available materials/required materials: Any items like text and visuals that must appear in the final and/or any resources the designer can draw upon to create the project.

How the design brief defines the design problem

The process of writing a design brief helps define the design problem. Writing the brief requires you to determine the important information needed to successfully complete the project. One important piece of information is the design constraints of the project. Design constraints are limits on what you can and cannot do. Designer Charles Eames put this best, saying that 'every design depends on its constraints' – meaning that you literally can't design something if you don't know what the constraints are. For instance, if the audience is defined by the brief as middle-aged women, the designer literally cannot make a design for teenage boys. If the brief asks for a package design, the client will not want a website no matter how well designed. These are extreme examples of ignoring constraints of course, but ignoring or not adhering to the constraints results in a weaker design.

Good design doesn't ignore constraints, it (ideally) addresses them in fresh and unexpected ways rather than working against them. Ignoring or dismissing the constraints in the brief is not creative, rather it is a sure step towards design failure. Ignoring the brief can happen surprisingly often, through misunderstanding or the urge to 'break the rules'. It's our observation that students often 'break the rules' when they are having trouble making a design look good. But you cannot solve a design challenge by changing it to something it is not.

Ignoring key parts of the brief does not solve a weak design, all this does is ensure the project does not meet the design challenge as defined. Therefore, thinking of design as a creative response to constraints is a more helpful mindset. When you receive a brief from your teacher (and later from clients) read it carefully and make sure you understand what each of the constraints are, then ask questions targeted to find out how far you can push them. Knowing this will enable you to produce a better design. However, be aware that there is sometimes a fine line between pushing the constraints and finding interesting solutions, and ignoring the rules and producing something that is not connected to the brief.

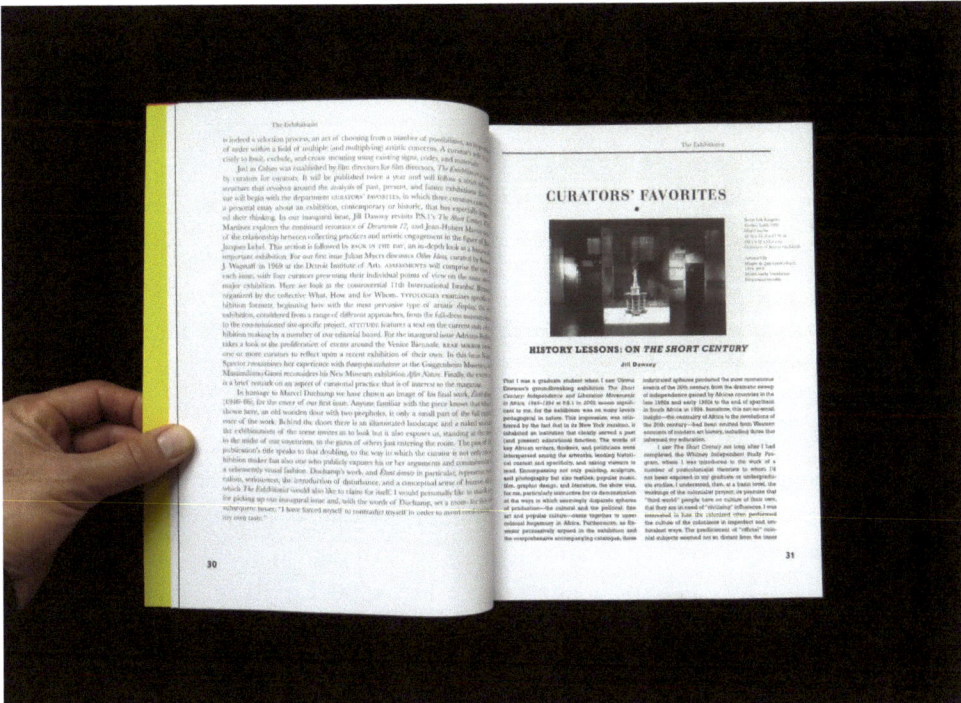

The design for this layout ignores the typesetting rules that captions should have their own column and not interfere with image space.

It may seem that when you are writing or completing a brief, leaving the constraints less defined is more helpful (because it leaves you more options, which seems like you can respond more creatively). Actually, the opposite is true. A vague (or no) set of constraints can create one of the most difficult design briefs to work from. When you write a brief for yourself, try to make it as clear and detailed as possible, remembering that even the tightest constraints may still be addressed in creative ways.

Loose versus tight briefs

Depending on how much input students must make to define their context, parameters and constraints, design school briefs can be measured on a continuum, from 'loose' to 'tight'. A very loose brief requires more input from a student, asking them to make decisions about items like content, goals, audience and formats. A very tight brief requires almost no student input and spells out in detail exactly what the content is, who the audience is, what you are making and when it is due. Most graphic design school briefs will be what we call 'blended', which means they fall somewhere between the two extremes. The amount of student input required in a brief is based on the course level and the desired learning outcomes that the teacher has in mind for the project.

A very loose brief sometimes approaches design in a more 'problem-based learning' way. Problem-based learning sets only a problem or prompt to be solved and leaves all the other parameters – including what is to be made – up to you. The looser the brief the more research is needed to define the context. In a very loose brief the final design will be judged on what you choose to make and why, in addition to the quality of the design. Another way a brief can be loose is to approach design as an exploration. In this kind of loose brief, process is highlighted and a polished final product is not the end goal or the main thing you will be assessed by. Instead, the instructor is looking for investigation into the visual, conceptual or technical aspect of the assignment.

Tight briefs are often used in early design school classes because they restrict your choices, and the less options you have the easier it is to design. Some briefs are prescribed to the point of providing all text and image content so that they function more like formal design exercises to help you understand basic design elements and principles. Tight briefs allow you to focus on a narrower context, which is helpful when you are learning, and makes it easier to understand when you have succeeded (or not).

Generally, as you advance in your studies and gain the basic conceptual and visual skills needed, the briefs you receive will become looser. This will free you up to shape your projects a little more. As you start to collect projects for your portfolio in advanced studio classes, this is especially important.

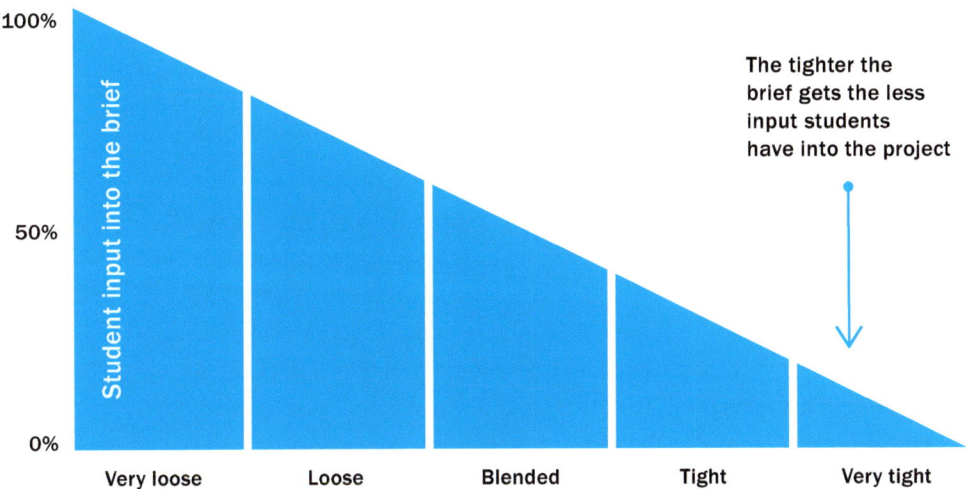

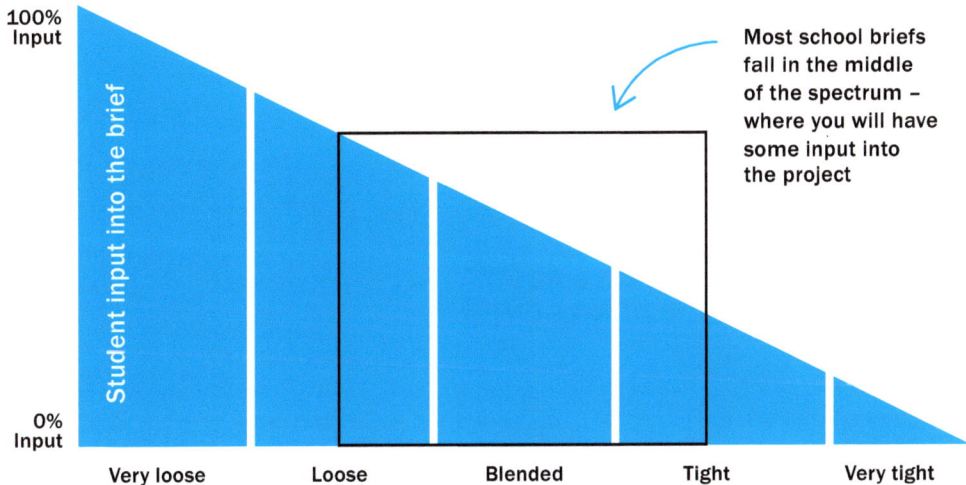

Top: Chart showing the spectrum of briefs from very loose to very tight.

Bottom: Chart showing where most design school briefs fall, into the middle of the spectrum.

Briefing in practice versus design school

Most design projects are completed in stages, step-by-step. The teacher lists what is to be done and when it is due. There is a focus on tools and materials in a school project brief because you are learning these as you produce the work.

A school brief might list an audience (this is especially common in a tight brief because all the criteria are constrained so the audience is factored in). Often, the audience is represented as a context rather than a specific set of demographics: for example, 'this book is something that would be sold in a museum gift shop'. A school brief often doesn't have a 'client' so it will instead list a purpose. The purpose can range from open ideas to specific direction. You could be given an open idea: 'make a sustainable design' or a specific direction: 'make a sustainable design packaging piece for a bar of soap'. The purpose will help you understand the criteria on which you will be judged. A big difference between professional practice and school is that in school you will often have to formulate the subject and content of the projects you make. Whereas in the professional world you will most likely be working with what is handed to you by the client. (For tips on making content see the box opposite).

A NOTE ABOUT CREATING CONTENT

Working designers are usually given content such as written copy, product names, market positioning, and imagery. In design school you will often have to be a client, writer, illustrator/photographer and marketer as well as a designer. Creating content can make projects more fun and personal, but you may not have the necessary skill sets (especially writing, which many design students struggle with). Making/writing good content is important to succeeding in design school because, to a certain extent, the more creative and well-executed this is, the better the final project will be. Graphic design teacher Rebecca Tegtmeyer uses a process to help her students generate written and visual content that you may find useful; read more in the following case study.

Project title: Making narratives: Title sequence project

Level and subject: Intermediate, Motion Design

Institution: Michigan State University, USA

Teacher: Rebecca Tegtmeyer

For this motion design project, students create a short title sequence based on 'an experience', using both copy and images. Rebecca walks her students through the following steps to create the visual and written content for the project:

Steps for creating content
>>

1. *Conduct research/reading to understand the task:* First it is important to truly understand what content you are tasked with creating. Rebecca's students do this by reading 'Having an Experience' from Dewey's book, *Art as Experience;* from this they make a list of the characteristics of an experience.

2. *Check/validate your ideas for content before committing to them:* Sharing your ideas helps to validate them (or not). Weak ideas can sound okay in your head but not when you speak them out loud to others. Rebecca's students write a list of personal experiences that meet the definition and choose one by discussing with the class. Rebecca stresses that students must be willing to put themselves out there and in turn be accepting of their peers during this process.

3. *Write a story:* A story can be the easiest form of writing because it taps into an essential designer skill set: storytelling. Rebecca explains that the act of writing is a design process method as well as an essential skill set; designers should strive to be good storytellers no matter the form (verbal, written or visual). For this project Rebecca's students write a story of 500 words or less.

4. *Translate the story into a mind map:* A story can be converted to visuals by using words from the story to create a mind map, which shows ideas and connections, both abstract and concrete. Rebecca suggests that her students list objects, places, people, events, feelings and anything else that represents the story using words only.

5. *Use a mind map to make a mood board.* Using the mind map words, make a mood board to generate/collect visuals to use in your design. Rebecca's students use the material from the mood board to make the key frames for their motion graphic, which is then paired with the written content from the story. At the end of this process, Rebecca's students' initial abstract ideas have a direct connection to both the written and the visual content.

You can try this process for generating written and visual content. Using stories helps you to write copy. Words from a story can be turned into visuals by being converted into mind maps. Mind maps can then be used to collect and generate visuals.

A professional briefing can range from a formal written document that functions like a contract, or an informal set of notes that are spoken or emailed. Often professional designers are called into a meeting, shown a presentation by the client that outlines a problem and then sent away without much information about what to do next. For large projects, a brief is often developed by marketing and strategy teams, and can be quite extensive, but for small jobs there may be nothing but a set of instructions hurriedly given to you. Even a fully researched brief does not break down the work for you the way the teacher does for you in design school. You may find yourself a little nostalgic for the clarity of a design school brief when you are out in the professional world.

Different kinds of design schools = different kinds of briefs

The kind of design school you attend will shape the kind of briefs you will be working with. We can define design schools on a spectrum from a more 'creative' to more 'professional' focus[1]. Where a school falls on this spectrum in part drives whether their briefs are tighter or looser, because the brief is integral to what students learn. Professionally focused schools – or what designer Michael Bierut calls 'portfolio' schools – focus on 'real world' skills, so many briefs are tight and the resulting student work looks like professional design projects. While More creatively focused schools – what Bierut calls 'process' schools – are more interested in fostering creative thinking over professional-looking projects, and so

The Academy of Art University is an example of a 'portfolio' school; students show their portfolios to employers at the end of their studies.

---

[1] Shel Perkins *Talent is not Enough* (2007).

tend to use looser, or exploratory briefs, which allow students to focus on process and problem-solving. The resulting student work might be less obviously commercial or polished.

All approaches on the continuum are valid; graduates of all kinds of schools end up working as designers, sometimes in the same studios. This is not a judgement about what approach works best. Rather, we find this is a helpful way of understanding why your school uses the kinds of briefs it does. The philosophy of the school aligns to the kind of work students do. This is just one reason why choosing the right kind of design school for you is important. You need to be on-board with your design school's philosophy or you will probably find it more difficult to work with the project briefs it sets for you.

UNDERSTANDING THE DESIGN PROBLEM

When you are given a design brief the first thing to do is to determine the relevant context. In graphic design, context means knowing as much as possible about the relevant circumstances surrounding a design project. To truly understand the context of each unique design problem you must understand as much as possible about the audience, as well as how, when, why and where the design will function.

The context of the design problem

Context can be physical, such as the location or environment for the final design. It can be production oriented, as in the type of media used, as well as budget oriented. Context involves human factors that can be cultural, behavioural, social or historical. It may sound like a monumental (even impossible) task to research all of this, but the trick is to confine yourself to understanding only the relevant aspects of the context.

'Relevant' means what is closely connected, or appropriate to, what is being done or considered. By reading the brief and asking questions, it should become clear that some aspects of the context are more important and are consequently more closely connected than others. Any other information that is not central to the design problem can then be considered a secondary concern (or perhaps even disregarded altogether.) For example, if you are tasked with designing a poster the most relevant questions that will reveal the context are:

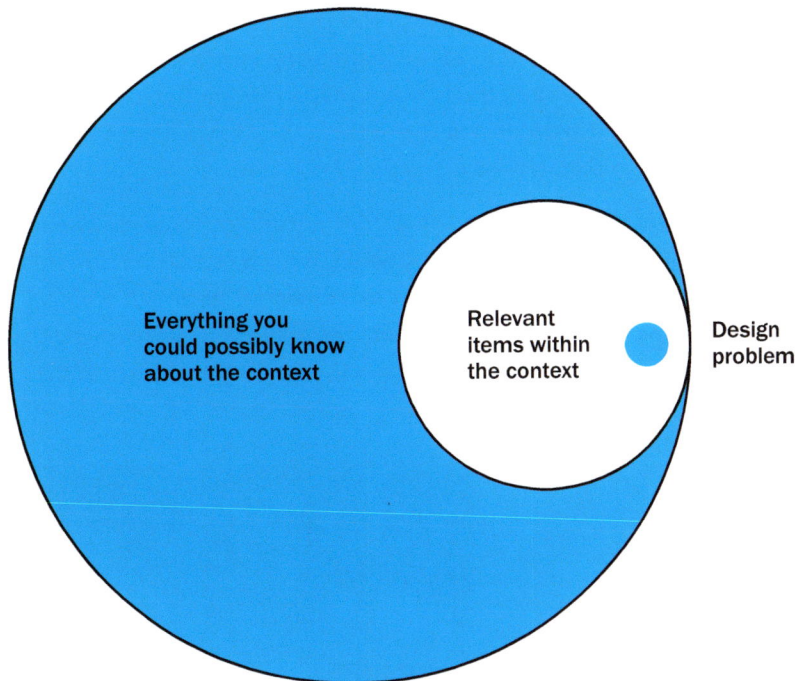

The Academy of Art University is an example of a 'portfolio' school; students show their portfolios to employers at the end of their studies.

Questions revealing context >>

- What is your subject matter?
- Who is your audience?
- How do people interact with this design?
- Where will the poster be located?
- What is the size of the design?
- Are there any supporting design items in the system?
- What are the materials?
- When is it due?

Context is interconnected and this is important in terms of design school projects where you may be asked to determine the subject matter. By choosing the subject matter, you will in turn be deciding the relevant context. Going back to the poster example above, if you chose an animated kids' film as the subject matter, you have determined the relevant audience: kids and their parents. Other people like college-aged males might be interested but so few of them that they are not a relevant audience and can therefore be disregarded.

Research about the context can come from 'outside' by researching visual and/or written information (articles, books, movies etc). Research can also be conducted from the 'inside' by experiencing the design problem first hand. This may mean going out into the world and experiencing environments or observing and talking with the people who are in the

Museums, boutique book stores, the world around you and architectural spaces are all good places to seek inspiration.

audience. It is also important to find previous examples of design related to your design problem and learn from them. By understanding what has been done previously you can be sure you do not recreate (or copy) designs, and you can take inspiration from their successes and failures.

Your goal in researching the context is to understand how the design you are creating will function in the world. This information will in turn allow you to create targeted, focused and successful design solutions. When you receive a brief ask yourself: Have I been provided with all of the information I need to understand the context? If not, then your first task is to conduct some research to find the relevant context.

Using the audience
to understand the design problem

The most important aspect of understanding context is the audience. These are the people who will experience and interact with your design. The way an audience interacts with a design will determine whether or not it is successful.

Always look at the design problem from the perspective of the audience as this will help you understand how to engage and communicate with them. Some of the relevant questions you might need to ask to understand the perspective of the audience are:

Where do they come into contact with the design?

What type of media do they consume?

What cultural, behavioural, social and historical factors are important to them?

Questions to understand audience <<

Understanding the audience is not simple, as every audience is made up of people and people are complicated[2]. It's possible that one audience will have ranges of ages, incomes, interests, etc. If that is the case the design challenge will be much more difficult. For example, let's pretend you have chosen an audience comprised of senior citizens and college students. Each of these two vastly different groups are in different stages of their life with different interests and mindsets. Each of these two different groups are engaged by different messaging, different media and different concepts.

Choosing a focused audience greatly increases your chances for understanding the design problem and creating viable and successful solutions. If the design brief does not tell you the specific audience, then start asking the important questions and find out who they are. If you are asked to define the audience try to be as specific as possible. Audiences may vary widely, but it is never 'everyone'. It is surprising

---

[2] It is not possible to go into detail about audience in this book because it's a huge subject and worthy of its own book, but there are many resources listed in Further Reading that are well worth investigating.

Senior

- Reads newspaper
- Looks at direct mail
- Conservative
- Likes to go on cruises

'I think about my family and the legacy I am leaving to them'

College Student

- Reads Twitter feed
- Looks at email
- Progressive
- Likes to go to mall

'I think about my friends and my next posts on social media.'

how often students will say just that. However, all this does is make the job of the designer harder. As with subject matter, when given a choice pick the audience carefully, and define it closely, as this can determine the success of your project.

Using the brief to define success

One of your first tasks when you get a brief is to determine what the instructor is looking for. Some things may be obvious; for example, a brief usually has specific directions about due dates and content, which must be followed to pass the project. A brief can also be used as a tool to define the project outcomes. Project outcomes are what you actually hope to achieve at the end of the project. By understanding context and requirements you can determine whether you have 'met the brief' (been successful) in the outcome when you complete your work. The brief sometimes contains everything you need to know, but sometimes the way a brief is written may create a sense of bewilderment – and this can be because your teacher wants you initially confused.

Some briefs are loose, requiring a lot of input from you as the student. These types of briefs do not fully scope the outcomes and requirements, so you may be confused and unsure of what a successful project looks like and what the outcome should be (at least in the beginning). In this kind of brief, it is only through investigation and exploration that you will arrive at success. To become a successful designer, you need to become comfortable with being unsure about some things as you work. Some things can only be known by trial and exploration. Start with questions and research, and understand that in a loose brief you are defining the outcomes on which you will be judged. The more specific and actionable you define the outcome and the steps to get there, the easier your job will be.

Some exploratory loose briefs do not require a final polished outcome. In these cases it is often not the destination (the final project) that is important but the journey (the exploration and iteration) that you take to get there. Success in these types of briefs simply means an in-depth and meaningful exploration of the concept or aesthetics. When working on this kind of brief it helps to think about the process as the product and as an end in itself.

In a tight brief the desired outcomes are usually very specifically scripted. There may be a timeline for producing the work and specific context will be provided (such as audience, media, placement, subject matter and content etc). Armed with this information, you will need to be very careful to follow direction. In a tight brief it is easier to understand when you have met the expectations, because you will either follow directions or you won't. In a tight brief your instructor is helping you to understand and to succeed by designating many of your choices in advance.

Ultimately, whether the brief is loose or tight, your design teacher wants you to succeed. If the brief lacks information or has an incomplete context or confusing directions, then seek clarification. Don't be afraid to ask for this. Teachers appreciate discussion and questions for clarification and often those discussions and questions can lead to answers that build a deeper understanding of the project, not just for you but also for other students in your class.

WHAT IS YOUR TEACHER LOOKING FOR?

In the following pages we have gathered examples of briefs ranging from loose to tight for this section. Each case study has teacher insights and information to help you get a better understanding of best practices for the different kinds of briefs. See more student examples and read each brief in its entirety at thegraphicdesignstudio.com

- Tight brief
- Explorative brief
- Blended brief
- Loose brief

Case study

A TIGHT BRIEF

A tight brief lists and prescribes specific goals and outcomes, creating a safe place for you to build a comfort level with specific design concepts and skills. Content may be student-sourced or provided by the teacher, but a tight brief will usually provide an audience, format and schedule.

Title: Digital Archive

Level & subject: Intermediate, Web Design

University: Monash University, Australia

Teacher: Tony Palmer

Deliverable: Multi-page website created by customising an existing Squarespace template.

——— PROJECT DESCRIPTION

To create a cohesive, interactive, professional-looking online portfolio using original images and copy. The images created for the archive must represent where the student is as a designer/illustrator/photographer and thinker. The design must demonstrate understanding of how to create an effective web presence.

——— HOW TO SUCCEED WITH THIS KIND OF BRIEF

Tony warns that students can overburden this kind of brief with needless complexity. For example, in this project creating images has a seductive lure, which becomes the student's initial and primary focus when they should be rapidly developing a basic

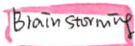

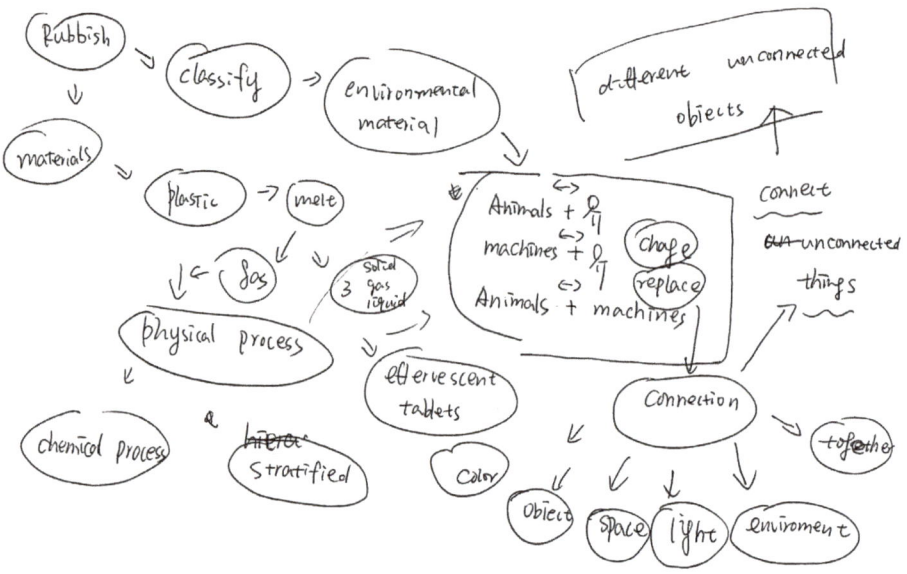

Student work by Yinzhi Chen

Student work by Yovina Kristiani Tandiharja

understanding of website page hierarchy. Tony suggests that the way to succeed is to focus on the skill or learning objective, not the parts you find the most compelling (like creating images). This will both save time and keep you focused on delivering what was asked of you.

Tony spends his instructional time in conversation and the participatory sketching-out of their website navigational structures to build the skill the brief is looking for students to demonstrate. To succeed in this kind of project pay attention to and align with what your teacher is focusing on during the critique, this will tell you the most important aspect of the project. In this brief, as with many tight brief projects, the expectations for deliverables are extensively laid out; innovating, or not following instructions, will result in failure.

——— WHAT YOUR TEACHER IS EXPECTING

Supply what has been requested by the brief, the way it is requested. Pay attention to the requirements. Although it can be tempting to work on the parts you find most interesting, keep your focus on achieving the objective of the project. If you are unsure about what that is, be guided by your teacher and by what they focus on during the critique.

Case study

AN EXPLORATIVE BRIEF

An explorative brief encourages students to explore aesthetic and/or technical possibilities within a defined parameter. The focus is on process rather than the outcomes being right or wrong.

Title: Media Queries Exercise

Level & subject: Intermediate, Web Design

University: California College of the Arts, USA

Teacher: Chris Hamamoto

Deliverables: A webpage linked to a personal homepage.

PROJECT DESCRIPTION

Using selected text from Lawrence Weiner's book *Statements,* students create a webpage that utilises media queries in CSS to create an interactive narrative. The narrative should unfold by resizing the browser, hiding/showing content, change in text size, colours, drop shadows, gradients, rotation and scale, etc. The goal is to create a more expressive browser experience instead of standard navigation centred around usability and clarity.

HOW TO SUCCEED WITH THIS KIND OF BRIEF

The brief is extremely short and direct, supplying very specific content and submission directions. Chris says this is on purpose; he tries to scale back the amount of content that students work with to encourage students to focus on aesthetics and interaction. To encourage students to try new ideas, Chris uses words like 'experimenting' and statements like 'and any other properties you can think of that you would not typically

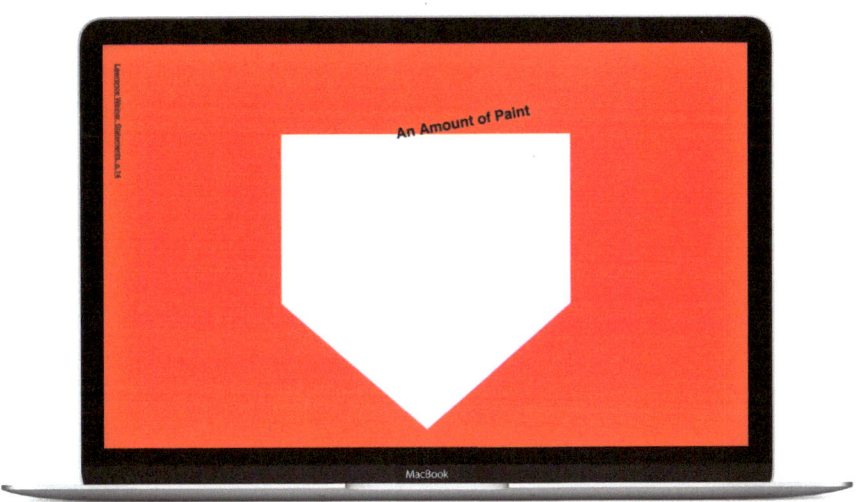

Top image: Student example.

Bottom image: Student example.

Student example.

manipulate'. These are prompts for students to approach the project with curiosity and scepticism. Removing expectations about success frees up exploration because we are more likely to try things we don't expect to work and be less worried when we fail. Being unafraid to fail is the key to good exploration.

When an assignment brief is built to facilitate exploration and not polished final outcomes, students often feel unsure about what the right answer should be. Chris says: 'Most often, students will be concerned with how their work is measured when there aren't well-established reference points that they can compare themselves to. To assuage this concern, I show examples of previous assignments, recommend using the source material as inspiration, encourage students that there isn't a right or wrong outcome, and make clear my expectations: that they learn the technical skill, and try something they may not have thought of before.' This brief is built to get students thinking freely and without concern for practicality. Chris ends his brief with good working advice for this kind of project: Push the limits of your exploration.

────── WHAT YOUR TEACHER IS EXPECTING

You are expected to play and explore. Work within the parameters but push the boundaries to see how far things might go – this is not the time to be tentative, so commit to the exploration.

Case study

A BLENDED BRIEF

A blended brief is a combination of loose and tight, where several of the parameters are defined by the student. The student input allows for variation in the process and the final design. Blended briefs are the most common type of design school brief.

Title: Material is the Message

Level & subject: Intermediate, Package Design

University: University of Illinois, USA

Teacher: Eric Benson

Deliverable: A PDF containing photographs of the original packaging and the final design with all components broken down.

—— PROJECT DESCRIPTION

Students design a package for a currently over-packaged technology item. Choosing an existing brand that can be sub-branded. The style, cost and size of the technology is open, but the new package design must be 'right-sized' (minimum ink and materials) and made only of recycled cardboard. The audience is the technology 'dabbler' market – people who are interested in sustainable products. The positioning (high or low end) is determined by each student.

HOW TO SUCCEED WITH THIS KIND OF BRIEF

Blended briefs require you to set some of the context for a project. Here, the students must choose the product to be packaged and the positioning (expensive high end, or cheap low end), while the teacher sets the materials (cardboard) and form (a package). Do not rush through your decisions to get to the designing, this can happen if you quickly get attached or excited about an idea. Eric recommends that students take some time to decide their inputs for the project in a practical, informed way. To help with this he emails the brief before class to allow time for the students to digest and to manage emotions like excitement, concern and feelings of being overwhelmed. This allows students to think and do their own cursory research before the briefing session, which can then help students feel more motivated and confident. Create some space for yourself to reflect and do some initial research. This will calm and focus your mind, helping you to make informed and practical choices that will set you up for maximum success.

Eric uses warm-up workshops and introductory exercises to help his students make informed decisions around materials and production methods before they decide what product they will choose to package. This type of guidance is not always provided by your teacher, so if you are thinking of tackling a new material or tool, try some low-impact 'throwaway' exercises on your own before you commit to your choices. Don't commit to any of the inputs you are putting into the brief until you are sure you can execute. Your chances of success are higher if you choose ideas, materials and tools you can use competently. At the same time be adventurous, if you don't try a new material or tool for fear it won't work out you might limit yourself unnecessarily.

WHAT YOUR TEACHER IS EXPECTING

Set the context for a project in a practical, informed way, do some research and thinking before you commit to your choices about you inputs for the brief. Use all the reference materials and evaluation criteria you are given to help you make good decisions for your brief.

Opposite page top left and right: Examples of student work Alyssa Sparacino.

Opposite page middle and bottom: Examples of student work Lemon Zhai.

Case study

A LOOSE BRIEF

A Loose Brief sets a problem or gives a prompt for the design and leaves all the other parameters up to the student. Having so much input enables students a high degree of control over the project context and design constraints.

Title: Capstone Project

Level & subject: Advanced/Social Responsibility

University: University of Maryland/U.S.A.

Teachers: Audra Buck-Coleman and Liese Zahabi

Deliverable: A presentation that identifies the message, audience and proposed artefacts is due in Semester 1. In Semester 2 students must define goals and schedule and complete the project. The final is artwork installed in a gallery exhibition, which is guest critiqued by an invited design jury before being refined and included in the senior portfolio.

PROJECT DESCRIPTION

Students create a design piece in response to the question: where does change need to occur in contemporary society and how might graphic design influence that change? Students must choose a social issue, situation or experience as the subject of the project then conduct secondary research and interviews to identify key insights before proceeding to design and production. The audience and deliverables are determined by the chosen subject.

The final is artwork installed in a gallery exhibition.

──── HOW TO SUCCEED WITH THIS KIND OF BRIEF

Audra suggests that to get the best result in this kind of brief, you should begin by committing to a subject or idea that has feasible design responses. She points out that the key to succeeding in this kind of project is anticipating limitations and potential production issues. While your teachers can predict possible roadblocks, you will still need to contend with unforeseen bumps in the road – the more realistic you are the easier these will be to overcome.

Liese instructs students in the second semester to divide the project up into pieces that make sense, and then create some kind of schedule with dates and milestones demonstrating how loose briefs need more planning than other kinds of projects.

Audra says that students are often uncertain about execution and how realistic the project should be. However, as students proceed through research they tend to have more specific questions such as about the audience and the production constraints. This shows the importance of asking questions. You can expect to ask broad questions at the beginning and more focused questions as you proceed.

Projects with open outcomes can be challenging to resolve neatly; both Audra and Liese believe that successful final projects come from a strong proposal and planning document. They suggest being specific with due dates and descriptions for each of the different components. According to Liese, 'the more detailed this is, the easier it will be for you to accomplish great things.'

──── WHAT YOUR TEACHER IS EXPECTING

The freedom of a loose brief demands more organisation. Apply discipline to stay on track and deliver successfully. Narrow the context and set realistic constraints at the beginning. Project planning is essential, so create timelines and establish milestones for yourself.

See more student examples and read each brief in its entirety at:
www.bloomsbury.com/the-graphic-design-process-9781350050785

The final is artwork installed in a gallery exhibition.

CHAPTER TWO

DESIGN

The design phase is often described as the most fun part of the design process because it is here that we get to 'ideate', or play with lots of ideas. Work you did during the Discover phase should have revealed several possible ways to approach the project, but there are still many possible ideas and solutions to explore.

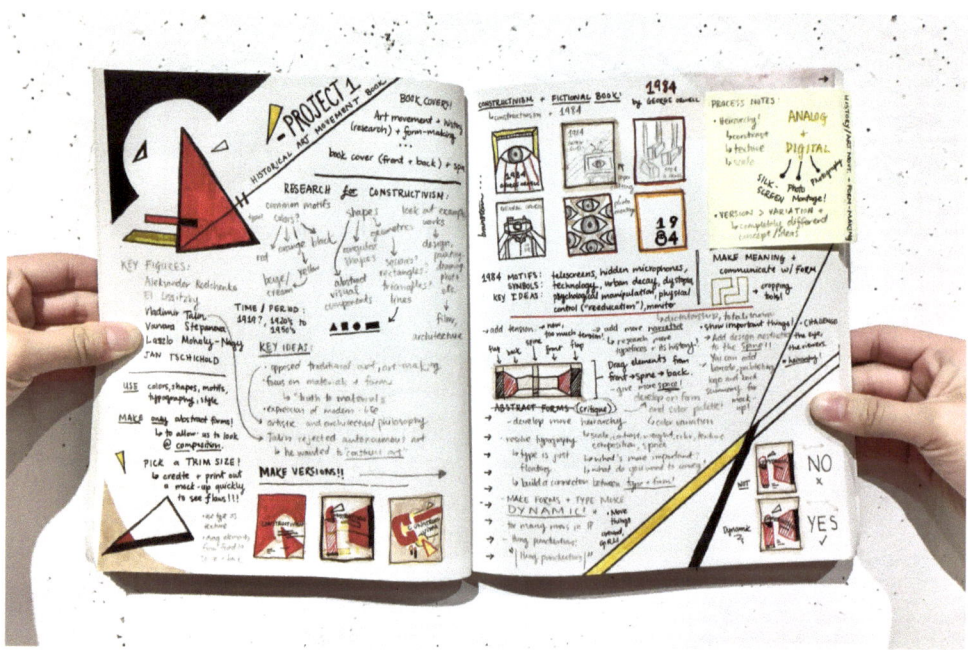

Pages from student Tracy Tran's sketchbook.

But the freedom and exploration that makes the design part of the creative process fun can also be a source of anxiety. It can be difficult to know where to start and choosing between many possibilities can be paralysing. There is potential to get stuck. In this phase, you want wide-ranging, uncensored exploration that links to the needs of the project. One of the things we will talk about in this chapter is creative thinking techniques to help your exploration.

DIVERGENT THINKING

The design phase relies on divergent thinking. Divergent thinking is the process of generating many different ideas. Divergent thinking is sometimes called 'creative thinking' or 'brainstorming'[1]. Designers use divergent thinking during the design phase to generate various options for solving conceptual and visual design problems. Good divergent thinking leads to good design and consists of generating multiple and recognisably different ideas, not just variations on one idea. After we generate many options we can then edit down and choose just the strongest ideas. Weak design comes from a lack of variation in ideas as well as a lack of quantity in ideas. If we don't have a wide range of ideas then we will be unable to edit or combine ideas. Editing and combining ideas can lead to better design solutions.

During divergent thinking, experienced designers do not think in terms of right or wrong answers. Instead they treat all ideas as equally potentially valid. Experienced designers know there will be some strong and some weak ideas. So, learn to take chances and be open during this phase of the design project; don't immediately edit out ideas.

Divergent thinking can be treated as a process using specific methods to generate results. This approach asks you to work through options rather than rely only on talent or chance. Talent and chance can help, and they can play a role in divergent thinking, but they cannot be solely relied upon when we are paid to be creative for a living.

---

1 Although 'brainstorming' is more accurately defined as a divergent thinking activity.

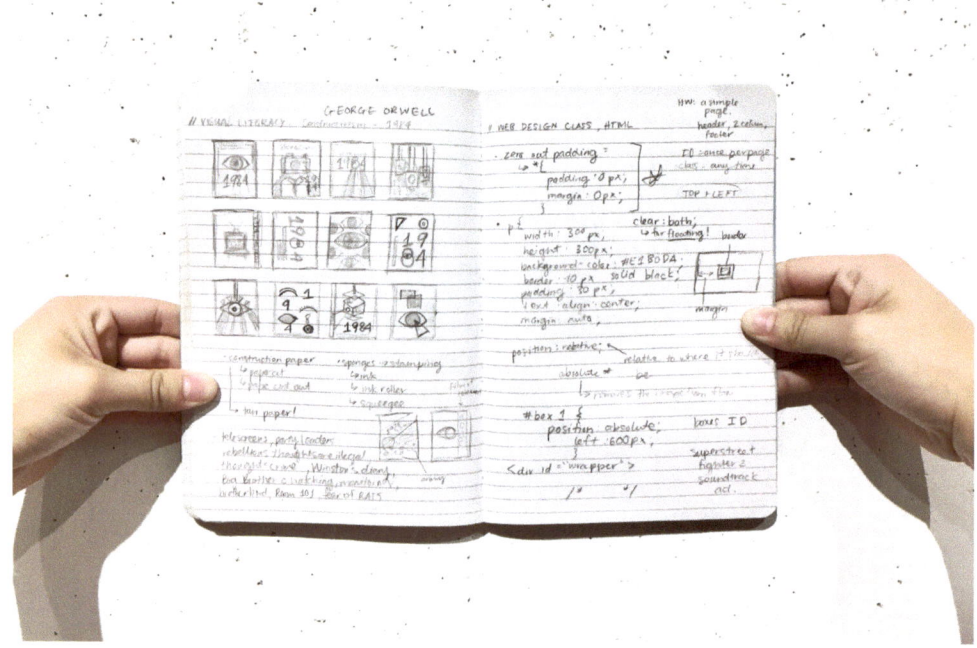

Images of student work, courtesy of Michael Worthington.

One difference between experienced designers and beginning designers is that they have spent years trying different types of methods and as a result have acquired a 'tool kit' of divergent thinking methods and techniques. This tool kit helps experienced designers generate a larger set of stronger ideas. For the beginning designer good divergent thinking can be more focused and productive when you are given methods to aid the process, and divergent thinking skills get stronger the more they are practised. The more you practise different methods of creative thinking, the larger your tool kit will become. Later in this chapter we will describe methods to help you practise divergent thinking effectively and get the most out of this stage of the design process.

What is your teacher looking for in the divergent thinking stage?

One of the main problems in this stage of the design process comes from misaligned expectations. Every student hears their teacher ask for a lot of ideas, however 'a lot' is subjective. It is likely that the number of ideas a teacher is looking for is higher than the number many students expect. Teachers look for a lot of ideas because they know from experience that out of any fifty ideas, there might only be three good ones. Out of those three good ideas, maybe one will actually be used. This means thirty initial ideas are better than ten, and the more ideas you have, the better your chances of success.

A common beginning design studio assignment asks students to come up with 50 ways to visually depict an object. This project is in part designed to show students how many possible solutions there really are to any given design project. In this situation students exhaust their initial generic and cliché ideas and must then figure out how to start to push past into new and interesting ones. For many beginning students, 50 seems like a lot until they work through the process of divergent thinking and surprise themselves by finding that they have more creative ideas then they thought possible. Always follow assignment instructions, but 50 different ideas is not a bad benchmark to aim for in any given assignment.

Another misunderstanding between teachers and students in this stage is what 'divergent' actually means. As we mentioned, divergent doesn't mean many slight variations on one idea, it means many different ideas. Teachers want to get as many possible visual and conceptual ideas on the table for discussion as possible. Meaning that the ideas produced in your divergent thinking stage should be distinctly different.

For example, let's say that in the initial sketching stage a student comes up with an idea or theme to use an apple as a logo. They then sketch the apple as red, then green, then a circular apple, then an oval apple, then with a leaf, then with a stem and finally a stem and a leaf. Essentially this student still only has one idea (an apple) shown in seven slightly different ways.

What should happen instead is that the student sketches the apple idea and then they move on to a complete different theme (not just a different fruit) as opposed to converging on the one apple idea and exploring the many ways an apple could be refined or represented. The selection of one idea then refining and exploring that one idea comes later after many different ideas have been put on the table.

So, count up your ideas and be honest with yourself about how many divergent ideas you actually have, and if it's not enough, keep going. There are always more ideas.

Example of seven non-divergent loosely sketched variations on apples.

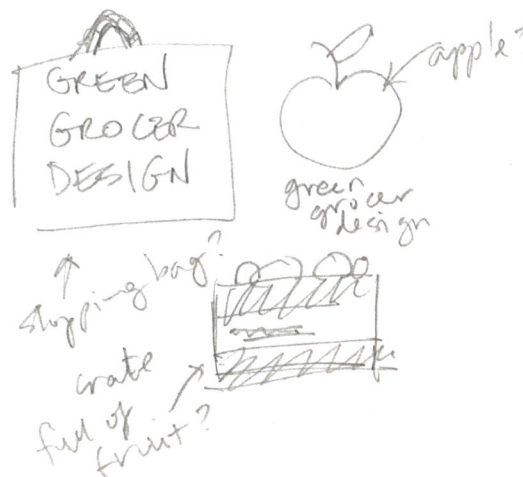

Example of three divergent loosely sketched themed ideas (an apple, a shopping bag and a crate).

Getting stuck during divergent thinking

Productive divergent thinking requires leaving aside a fear of being wrong; it also means generating a lot of ideas fairly quickly, and for these reasons this can be the first place in the design process that designers get stuck. Getting 'stuck' means failing to progress a design in some way, and this tends to happen more through the start and middle of a project than at the end. At the beginning of a project, watch out for the heavy and overly stressful feeling that you are making big conceptual and visual decisions that will have a far-reaching impact on the design and which cannot be undone. You are not committing to anything yet. Being stuck might mean not being able to generate ideas, or not being able to choose between ideas. Students most often describe the feeling of being stuck as being 'blocked' or 'frozen'. We call this feeling 'stuckness',[2] and it is the designer equivalent of 'writer's block'.

---

2 We take the term 'stuckness' along with her characterisation of being 'fixated' and the idea of the 'stop-start' design process from Avagail Sach's 1999 research paper *'Stuckness' in the design studio*.

It can be difficult to know the difference between the normal design process and stuckness. Design can be a stop-start process; feeling unsure, or not knowing the best option to choose is common. It is how long the struggle lasts and how repetitious and cliché the ideas are that characterises actual stuckness. Experienced designers have completed the design process many more times than beginners, and therefore have a better understanding of what is 'normal'. This is why a teacher may not consider that a student is stuck, even if from the student's perspective they are stuck. For a teacher it is normal to have a period of time where good ideas are not flowing easily, and they know that this will usually pass. Students must work past the point of being stuck.

Stuckness can be a result of not looking at a design problem from many perspectives, but it can also come from being in a design programme and studio classroom. Students are tasked with designing while they are learning to design. Learning by doing can be difficult and a bit scary (ask anyone who has learned how to ski). Learning new software, terminology, skills and techniques while creating class work is a difficult task. Additionally, a studio class, like the professional world, forces you to move briskly along, producing and showing ideas. Limited time to accomplish a complicated activity, with the pressure of deadlines and showing your work, means there is a greater possibility of getting overwhelmed, and consequently, of getting stuck.

In the divergent thinking stage we often experience getting stuck as an inability to generate ideas. Alternatively, and more dangerously, we may get fixated: which means not being able to move past one or two ideas. This can happen when a fairly good idea is produced early on in the process and the project feels 'solved'. Or the designer may circle around and make small variations of one, or even a few, not so great ideas. If you find yourself repeating the same kind of sketch over and over (like the apple example), you are probably a bit stuck.

In this example you can see that the student has essentially three ideas, even though there are 16 sketches. This example is from our student Sarah Mease. Sarah ultimately succeeded with this project through a willingness to throw out ideas and start again. Sarah says as difficult as this experience was, getting through the stuckness made her a stronger designer.

The good news is that we rarely see cases of serious stuckness that result in failure. There is almost always a way out of stuckness, it does not necessarily doom you or your project to failure. However, getting stuck may limit the amount of ideas you generate and this can put the quality of the final project at risk. Stuckness will happen to you, so finding ways to work around it is essential.

What can you do about stuckness?

Firstly, reframe what you are feeling. Being stuck is sometimes a result of simply being in a design studio class and being asked to perform creatively on demand. Being stuck is a normal part of the design process itself, it is not because you are failing. Statistically it is very unlikely that you have a 'terminal' case, so it's vital you keep moving and not stop, because then you will fail.

One of the key ways to avoid getting stuck when you start a project is to work methodically, using divergent thinking techniques rather than sitting around and waiting for inspiration to strike and 'unfreeze' you. The biggest danger in stuckness at the beginning of a project is fixation and repetition, and this can happen even when you are diligently working and using divergent thinking strategies. There are a variety of strategies you can use to get unstuck, all of them are focused on breaking the cycle, and resetting your mind to see new perspectives and ways of solving the design challenge.

Breaking the cycle can happen in literally hundreds of ways, from physically changing your location, to getting input from others. Finding the methods for getting unstuck that works for you comes from simply trying out various methods. Here is a small sample of common methods that designers use to get unstuck:

Deep freeze: This is an idea stolen from the writer Stephen King. The writer recommends mentally filing ideas away in a 'freezer' so that we 'kill' them without actually 'killing' them. The idea is that our brain then thinks of the ideas as 'done', without having to let go entirely – which can be difficult – and this frees us up to move onto new things. This idea is particularly helpful when you are fixated on one idea. Think to yourself: 'It's a good idea, I will preserve it in the deep freezer, and move on, I can always come back and get it later.'

Get physical: Physical change to the body can also free up the mind. For example, taking a shower will reduce the sensory intake of your brain and allow you to focus inwards, uncluttering your mind and freeing it up to think of new things. Getting up earlier in the day, or exercising, or taking a new route home can change the pattern of your day too, which has the same effect.

Methods for getting unstuck <<

Take a break: Your subconscious mind will keep working on a problem, and sometimes work more quickly if you leave it alone to work. To do this, distract your mind with something else, like watching a movie, or playing with a child, or just going for a walk. Or try putting your mind in a new space: Read an article, go to a new museum, listen to a new piece of music – anything novel that will divert your mind. If you use this method, be sure to come back to the work in a timely manner or you might then have issues around getting your work done within the deadline.

When you are trying to solve a design problem tray putting your ideas in the deep freeze, doing some exercise, or taking a break.

TECHNIQUES FOR GENERATING IDEAS

There are numerous books and articles about creative blocks and where creative ideas come from (and how to get unstuck). We also created a tool for beginning designers to help them with divergent thinking – you can find details of our tool in the Further Reading chapter. In this section we will present some of our favourite methods for generating ideas.

Creative Connection Cards exist as a deck of 107 cards. Creative Connection App exists as an iOS app.

Defining keywords

Ideally, research using the brief will provide insights about the design problem. One of the ways designers convert research and insights into divergent visual ideas is through developing a set of keywords. Keywords are a way to encapsulate an entire project, making it concise and manageable. For this reason, in the professional world keywords are often included in a brief to help drive the overall direction of a project.

Keywords are single words that act as guides for generating ideas; they represent the core of the project and can be drawn from the insights and the goals as outlined in the brief. Designers usually start with a long list of possible words that they gather as they research and then narrow them down to the most useful ones. Some designers use as few as one keyword, but we recommend using three. Three keywords provide a wide enough range to guide the project without becoming overwhelming and confusing.

Good keywords are visual or have visual possibilities. They are specific, not generic. For example, the word 'modern' is generic and fairly open to interpretation, whereas the word 'sterile' describes a certain kind of modern. So, 'sterile' is a better keyword than 'modern' if it aligns to the project goals.

Using architecture as an example, we could think of the image on the left as 'modern' and the image on the right as 'sterile'. Both are 'modern' in that they are both white and clean looking. At the same time, these are quite different images with different meanings, showing how the word 'sterile' will evoke a more specific association in the mind of the viewer.

It can be helpful to start from the generic and work to the specific qualities you are trying to embody in a keyword. For example, 'beautiful' could be made more specific by using 'ornate' or 'detailed'– each word is more descriptive and will produce more possibilities. It is helpful to choose keywords that will set your project apart. This can be best done by choosing words that are as specific to the true meaning you are trying to express, and as specific to the design goal as possible.

When teachers ask for words that are visual or have visual possibilities, this means using words that are evocative. So think in terms of texture, movement and dimension as well as colour, brightness and feeling. Keywords can be emotive and should be open to possibilities, not limiting, so if one or more of the keywords don't work then reach for other possibilities. (You can see how the thesaurus is one of the designer's best friends in the search for keywords.)

It can be helpful to think of keywords and how well they will perform for you by using them in this phrase: *'I want to design something that feels (insert key word here).'* As designers, we are looking to create an emotional connection and feeling in the minds of the viewers. So think of keywords from the perspective of what emotions and ideas they have the ability to evoke in the audience.

Defining a set of keywords is a useful thing to do for every design project. It is a tool that can be used in other various divergent thinking methods, such as mood boards and mind maps.

Conducting visual research based on keywords

Design exploration often begins with visual research. Visual research is a process of looking to the world around us, including other pieces of design, to provide inspiration for new ideas. All design is derivative in some way. Sometimes it is inspired by other design, or by architecture, marks on a wall, a photograph, whatever.

One way of targeting visual research, and finding the most helpful inspiration, is by using keywords to find and collect visual examples. We call these visual examples 'pulls' because great design is built (or 'pulled') from the work that came before it. Designers can 'pull' ideas from visual inspiration to begin design exploration.

Opposite page top: Examples of images related to the keyword 'bold'.

Opposite page bottom: Examples of images related to the keyword 'connected'.

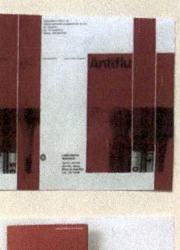

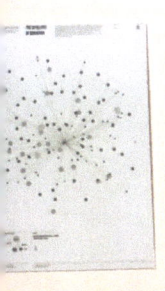
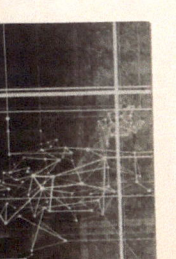
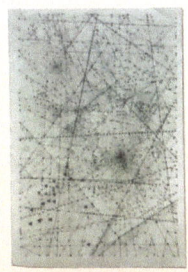
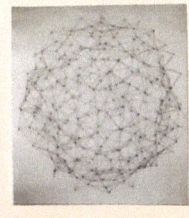
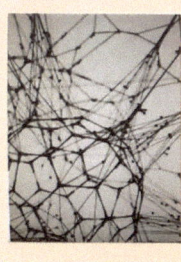
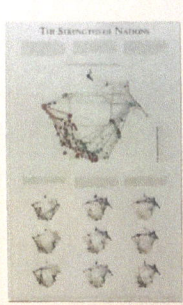
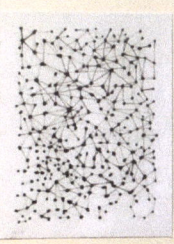
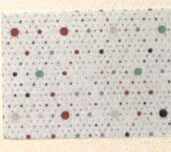

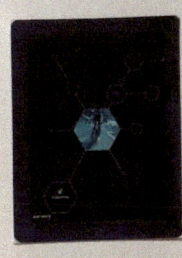

Discover > **Design** > Develop > Deploy

A pull can be another piece of design, a photograph, an illustration, typography, or colour palettes, or anything that visually aligns with a keyword. Pulls act like guides to help explore design ideas. They are visual sparks, not something to copy. Using pulls to come up with design ideas is a fluid process of realigning, reworking, reinventing and recombining ideas to meet the specific design goals outlined in the brief.

When searching for pulls, look for visual elements that connect to the keyword. The connections can be loosely related or obvious. Elements like composition, colour, scale, techniques and the like, which can be directly 'pulled out' can be used as a starting point for a new idea. Not all pulls are created equal, one pull might generate a number of ideas while another may have only one useable idea. The goal is to collect as many varied and interesting pulls that match the keywords as possible. The more ideas you gather as pulls, the more divergent concepts and visuals you will be able to make. Remember that a pull, like a keyword, should not be limiting. Instead, pulls should be open to interpretation and might spark multiple directions.

As an example, let's say the brief and initial research leads to using the word 'evolve' as a keyword. To start using this keyword to collect pulls we can begin by looking it up in the dictionary.

Here is the definition for evolve: '…develop gradually, especially from a simple to a more complex form'. Then the synonyms: '…develop, progress, advance; mature, grow, expand, spread; alter, change, transform, adapt, metamorphose'.

Notice that there are a number of synonyms for 'evolve' that have visual possibilities along with the definition. When gathering pulls, keep all of the synonyms and definitions of the particular keyword in mind. While it's not a good idea to go too far off on a tangent and alter the original meaning, all of the different visual angles and trajectories that a word may inspire should be explored. Allowing the word to branch out to broader meanings via the synonyms will bring in new ideas and perspectives. In this way you can see how there can be a huge variety of divergent visual ideas from one keyword.

An example of a pull that could be seen to represent the keyword 'evolve'.

As designers grow more skilful, they start to translate the non-graphic design things they see around them into graphic design.

Designers tend to collect visual things, often creating a large catalogue of inspiration from the world all around them on the walls, on their computers, or in books and magazines. Beginning designers will benefit from initially collecting graphic design pulls, then adding in pulls that are visuals of other kinds (such as architecture, photography, etc). This strategy provides a strong base from which to start exploring.

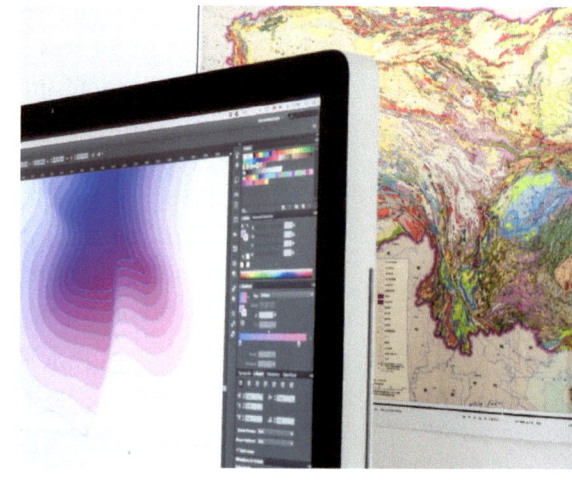

This design is inspired by geology and maps, and you can see the direct connection between the images of the things the designer has looked at (images above) and visual language that was developed for the project (images below). Design by Necon, reproduced with permission.

Using mood boards

Mood boards are a tool for collecting and displaying visual inspiration for a project. Designers select and arrange images on a mood board to communicate the design goals of the project. Mood boards can be used to help clients understand a design direction, and are most often used by designers during the design exploration process.

Fill mood boards with useful images, not just inspirational images.

Typically, mood boards are filled with 'inspirational images', which might be looked at, but not actively used to generate ideas. Or designers may fill a wall with 'inspiration' as they work to keep them in the right 'visual mood'. Just collecting and looking at visual research is not as useful a method as it could be. Pulls make mood boards more active in the design exploration process, because ideas are being actively 'pulled out' of each visual placed on the mood board.

We recommend you use one moodboard per keyword. Ten or more pulls usually generates enough ideas, the more pulls the more potential ideas. Individual mood boards should be added to, and changed, during the course of design exploration. Each pull should have a reason to be on the board – it should trigger a new idea, and it is best not to repeat pulls with the same content or idea. For example, if your keyword is 'diffuse' and you have a pull that shows something blurry, then do not show another pull with something blurry – you only need to show an inspiring idea once on a mood board.

With each pull there should be a brief written description of exactly what was inspiring about it. When the sketching part of design exploration begins, these notes serve as a reminder about what was inspiring and how the idea connects to the keyword. This keeps idea generation focused on the brief.

 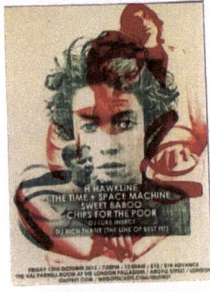    

Here is a sample mood board with corresponding pulls and notes with each pull for the word 'overlap'.

Only include good graphic design and quality pulls on a mood board. Bad design like poor colour palettes, low-quality imagery and weak typography are not inspiring and should not be used to pull ideas from. After all, great dishes come from great ingredients.

Using keywords and pulls to sketch ideas

The design exploration phase of the design process is where you can have fun because it involves investigating visual ideas – a lot of them. The best way to do this is by sketching. Devoting the appropriate time and energy to sketching is the key to successful design exploration and will pay off in a better project.

Because each mood board is based on a related keyword you can feel confident that the ideas they spark will automatically be linked to the goals as outlined in the design brief. A designer can be more confident during exploration when they don't have to worry if visual exploration is on target. If enough time and care is taken collecting pulls to construct the mood boards, there should be a lot of ideas to start visually exploring. Start sketching by looking at the pulls on the mood boards. Read the notes detailing what was inspiring about each pull. Look at, analyse and evaluate what is successful from each of the pulls. Use this information to spark ideas and start sketching.

 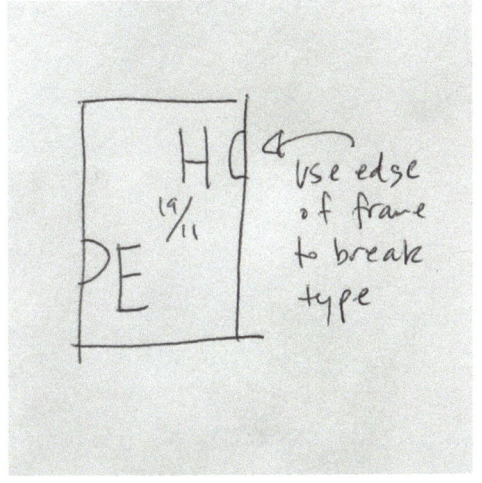

Here is a pin from the overlay board and the sketch it inspired. See how the forms have sparked an idea for a typographic treatment idea.

Remember, what makes each design solution different is the perspective of the designer. It is the combination of your visual decisions based on what the pull inspires that creates new visual ideas. The same designer looking at the same pulls and having the same keywords would find different visual elements and ideas because they have a different perspective. So explore. Feel free to edit and combine ideas. Let ideas take you to new places. Strive to make engaging and exciting things.

Mind mapping and semiotics

A mind map is a creative thinking tool that maps word associations around a central concept. The action of writing words and ideas down means you can let them go and move on, discarding the obvious 'bad' ideas to get to new and more interesting ones.

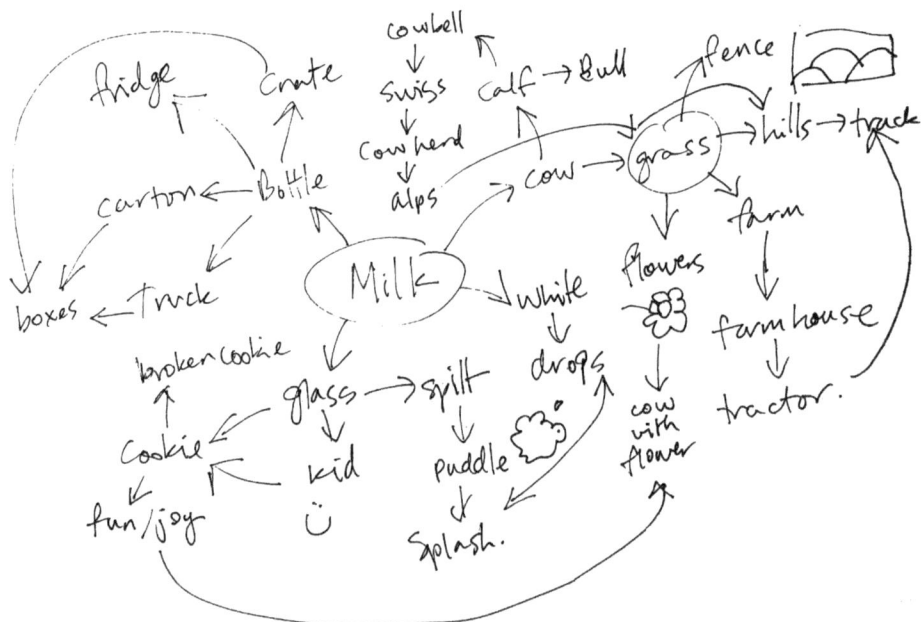

Begin a mind map by writing a word or phrase in a circle, and then draw 'branches' out from that circle.

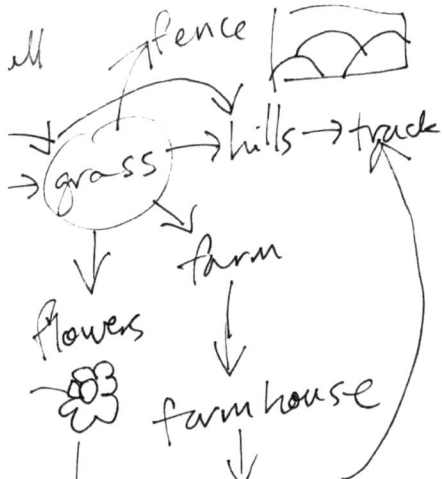
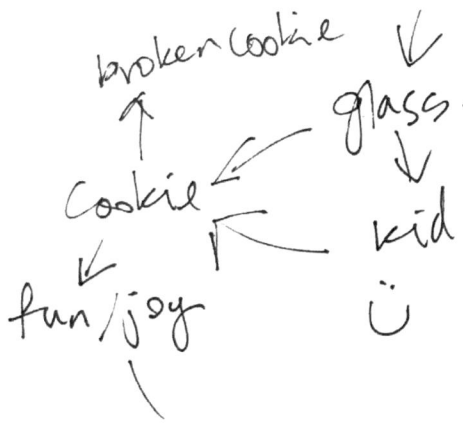

At the ends of the branches list the words/phrases/imagery that are associated. You can write or draw, or both.

A mind map isn't linear so when your thoughts are exhausted on one branch, start another. You can switch from branch to branch and even connect two (or more) branches together to form a new idea.

Some designers use different colours to track themes, but you can work in black and white if you prefer. There are digital mind mapping tools available, but we find that pen and paper are better because they are free flowing.

By making a mind map you are conducting what is called a 'semiotic exploration'. Semiotics is the study of how humans attach meaning to words and images. Designers manipulate words and images to create meaning, so we deal in semiotics all the time. Understanding semiotics is useful for generating ideas and making better mind maps (as well as being a designer). There is no room in this book for a deep dive into semiotics so we will just outline the main idea.[3]

Words are just sounds when we speak them, but once meaning is attached to them, they become what we call in semiotics: 'signs'. A sign

---

3 See Further Reading for more resources on this topic.

is an idea in our mind. Signs are formed by shared language and culture and help us communicate because we all agree on the meaning of a given sign. People from different cultures can often have trouble understanding each other because of not sharing the same meaning behind signs. Images can be signs too.

The word apple is associated with fruit and the technology company, while the apple logo is an example of an image that has become a sign.

Each person will then connect their own meanings to a sign based on their own experiences. This means signs can have multiple meanings, some shared, and some not. This is especially true of images because they are not as specific as words.

If you know how your audience sees the world, you can speak to them more effectively by using the right signs. The more specific a sign is, the better it will communicate to the audience but the more it could be

For example, to a person raised within Judaeo-Christian culture an apple has associations with sin and temptation that someone who was raised in a Buddhist culture won't necessarily share. Someone who was raised on an apple farm will probably have personal associations to apples, based on picking apples and endlessly being fed apple pie, which most other people will not share at all.

misunderstood by those outside the audience. If the sign is too obscure, the audience will miss the meaning. The trick lies in creating what has been called the 'inevitable surprise', a connection between sign and meaning that is not obvious or tired (i.e. a cliché), creating surprise and delight in the mind of the viewer. This kind of idea is what design teachers often call 'fresh': something new, novel, unexpected and memorable. So, if you create a logo for an apple-picking farm using an apple, you will not surprise anyone. If you make a logo for an apple-picking farm using a guitar, you may have something surprising.

When you are mind mapping you can reveal the meanings and the connections of signs. Some will be obvious, others deeply buried in your unconscious. Because a mind map makes these connections visual, it allows you access to ideas you may not previously have been able to think of (because you could literally not see them).

DESIGN EXPLORATION USING SKETCHES AND DRAFTS

Design exploration needs speed and volume, as well as detail and accuracy, so designers break up sketching into two types: 'loose' and 'tight' sketches.

Loose sketches

Loose sketching allows designers to generate more ideas, faster. Loose sketches do not contain a lot of detail or accuracy; they are like notes for ideas. Working with a pencil (or pen) on paper creates 'loose' quick, non-detailed sketches, allowing ideas to flow uninhibited. The trick to creating effective loose sketches is to represent the ideas well enough that they can be recognised and developed into 'tight' sketches at a later time. If we look back at loose sketches and have no idea what we were thinking, then the sketch is basically useless.

All ideas are in play during loose sketching. Don't edit, just think it—then sketch it. Be quick, take only enough time to represent the idea, then move on. It helps to make notes to remind yourself what the idea is about, these can be used as a reminder later for creating tight sketches. Don't judge ideas in their infancy; initial ideas are not final. Loose sketches will be revisited later to decide on their merit. Make a sketch and move on to the next one.

After a lot of loose sketching, as the design exploration process develops, it's important to start making decisions and to converge on the best ideas. Making decisions means putting some ideas aside, and then focusing and refining other ideas while still in sketch form. To do this work designers evaluate, choose, connect and combine ideas from loose sketches (as we mentioned, some of the best ideas come from editing and combining ideas). Once you have many loose sketches you can move on to create 'tight' sketches.

Here are some good loose sketching examples for a poster project. Student work by Jacob Ricks.

Tight sketches

Tight sketches should go into more detail than loose sketches by showing the compositions and representing details more accurately. Tight sketches are not necessarily beautifully crafted or highly detailed, but they do refine and start to show generally how the idea will work by including all the required elements for the design. Choose only the best loose sketches to be made into tight sketches. This selection process is called 'convergent thinking' and is used to force decisions and eliminate ideas that are not as strong. To decide what to transfer to tighter sketches, look through the loose sketches to find the 'gems' or possibilities. Decide which ideas resonate and have potential, then continue to look for the ways these ideas could be combined.

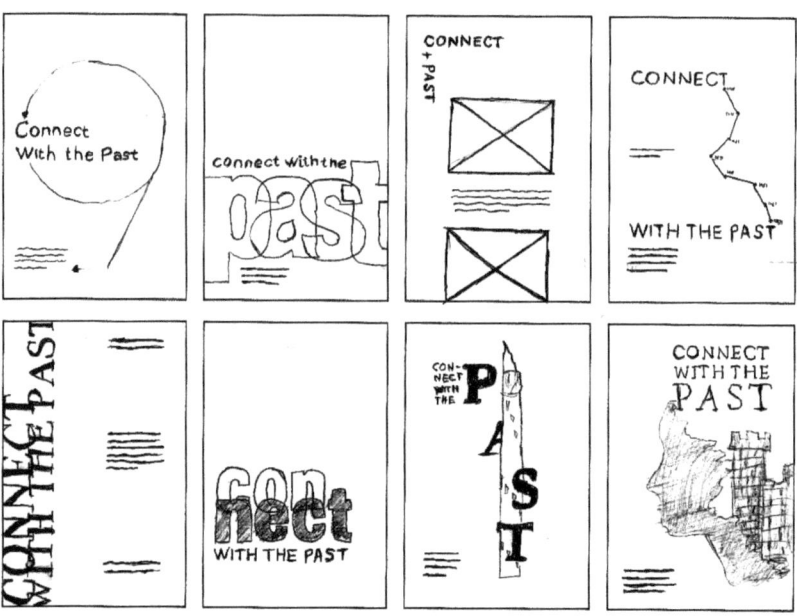

In the poster example above notice the difference in the level of detail and polish between the initial loose sketches and the tight sketches. Also notice that there are more loose sketches than tight ones, because they are initial ideas and faster to represent. Student work by Jacob Ricks.

It is a good idea to invite critique about loose sketches from fellow students before you show them to your teacher. Your peers can help to validate or challenge any loose sketch ideas that you plan to make into tight sketches. Talking with others will force you to describe and evaluate your ideas in words and see if other designers understand and (hopefully) get excited by your ideas.

Moving back and forth between pen and computer

We deliberately described how to sketch properly with pen and paper before talking about the computer, because sketching with a pen and paper supports a more fluid process. A pen doesn't have any pre-existing form except the thickness and colour of the line, and this allows us to produce a greater range of ideas. More ideas are always good.

Graphic design software applications are restrictive. They have built in shapes like circles and squares which although easy to use, can restrict experimentation. Computer-generated shapes are unfortunately

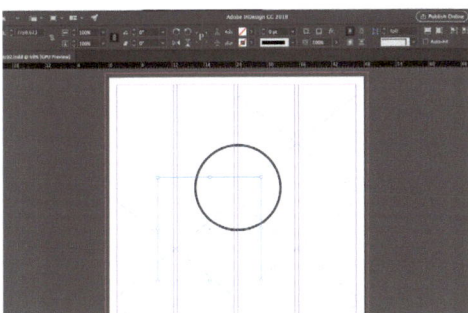

Contrast using pen and paper with sketching on the computer where you must: choose an application, open a file, manipulate a mouse (or pen and tablet), select a tool, name and save before working. With a pen, very little gets between your brain and the paper.

perfect, and this restricts happy accidents (which is where some of the best ideas can come from). Using a computer instead of a pen forces us into decisions about how things will look before our ideas are fully formed.

We recommend you start working on ideas with a pen and paper.[4] Starting with a pen and paper does not mean we leave the computer out of the design process. The disadvantages of computers provide some

Ironically a 'handmade' solution can benefit most from using a computer, as it allows us to undo and perfect handwork in a way a pen and paper cannot.

obvious advantages. With a computer we can make a move, assess it and move again, then repeat as many times as we like. The computer helps us try out lots of ideas this way, and to quickly see whether they will work so we don't waste time on unviable ideas.

At what point you bring the computer into this part of the process is up to you, but we recommend using pen and paper first and then moving the best ideas to rough computer drafts. We recommend going back to pen and paper when computer drafts show an idea won't work and/or new ideas need to be generated. Our only hard and fast rules are don't start on the computer, and don't design only on the computer.

---

4   A pen can be a pencil, crayon, brush or whatever you prefer/feel comfortable with.

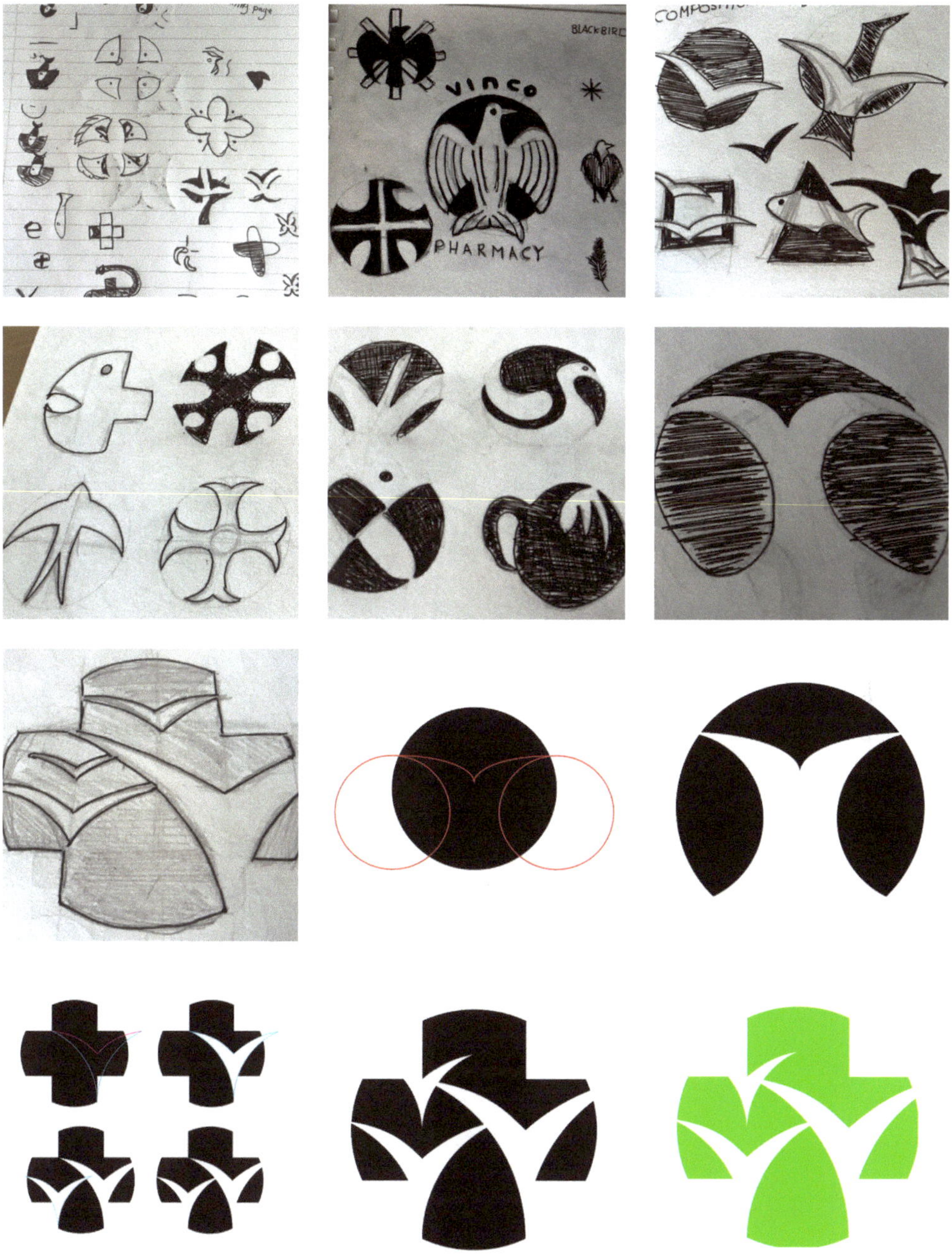

This sequence of images shows the steps from loose sketching through tight sketching into computer roughs.

Discover > **Design** > Develop > Deploy

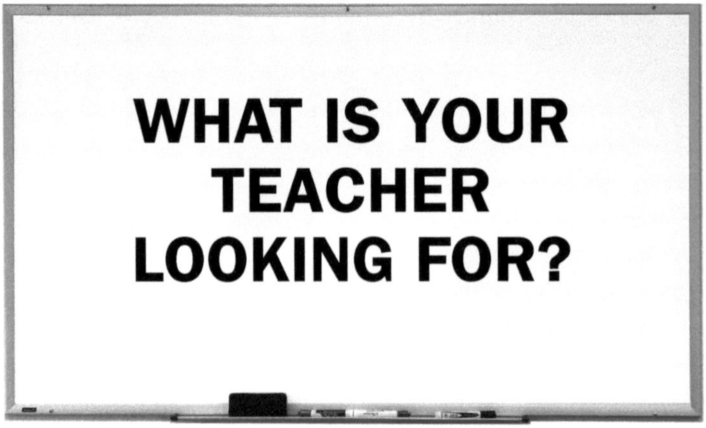

WHAT IS YOUR TEACHER LOOKING FOR?

In the following pages we have gathered examples working through the design phase. Each case study has teacher insights and information to help you better understand best practices for generating divergent ideas.

- Divergent thinking
- Loose sketches
- Tight sketches

Case study

DIVERGENT THINKING

Divergent thinking consists of playing with, and investigating ideas, using the project parameters to help you to generate as many potential visual and conceptual ideas as possible.

Title: Template for image-making

Level & subject: Introductory, Fundamentals of Design

University: California College of the Arts, USA

Teacher: Jon Sueda

Deliverable: A physical template that is constructed from geometric forms and has the capacity to create clean, precise, lines and shapes. A set of one-colour sketches completed by hand using the template, utilising pens of various thickness.

—— PROJECT DESCRIPTION

This project is set up to develop the student's ability to explore divergent ideas and forms in a simple way. Students first make a plastic template to use as a physical mark-making tool and then create a set of drawings using the template (see image on the following page). A template allows students a clearly defined space from which to explore form, language, communication and storytelling. Multiple divergent formal explorations result from quite restrictive templates, which shows students how many ideas can be developed within a seemingly strict set of limitations.

Students first make a physical template.

HOW TO SUCCEED WITH DIVERGENT THINKING

Jon emphasises that the key to divergent thinking is to focus on process rather than result. In this case, you are investigating process and having the mindset of a 'continuous' project or process that might have no end, is the best way to approach it. This 'continuous' mindset is important for divergent thinking. Approaching an exploration by creating form or ideas simply to see what happens, and where they lead, allows you to work without being bound or restricted to one idea.

It can be a scary proposition to be told to simply 'explore form', and Jon speaks directly to the issues students face when given this type of project, saying: 'Students don't see the value in formal exploration for its own sake. They want a process to quickly add up to something practical or useful that is measurable in some way.' However, new ideas and visual forms can happen when there is time in a project given to open divergent exploration. Without this step in the process, design can become clichéd and expected.

Students can 'get stuck' or 'run out of ideas' when divergent thinking is required. Jon says the best way to get unstuck is to: 'Embrace restrictions and limitations. When you create parameters to an investigation it helps one to create the rules of a game and allows you to be creative within those rules.' It may seem contradictory to say that restrictions can create possibility, but Jon is showing how important design constraints are. When designers are faced with too many choices or options, it is more difficult to focus and produce work; after all, where do you go when you can go anywhere? People in this situation are usually indecisive and don't go anywhere (i.e. get stuck). Constraining choices helps us choose.

Jon sets the parameters of this project by forcing students to make a template and then use only that template to create forms. Those limitations allow students a place with a clear defined space to play within. Within these limitations the students' only task is to generate more and more ideas. Sueda says: 'In the end, it's about making more, and making your way out of being stuck.'

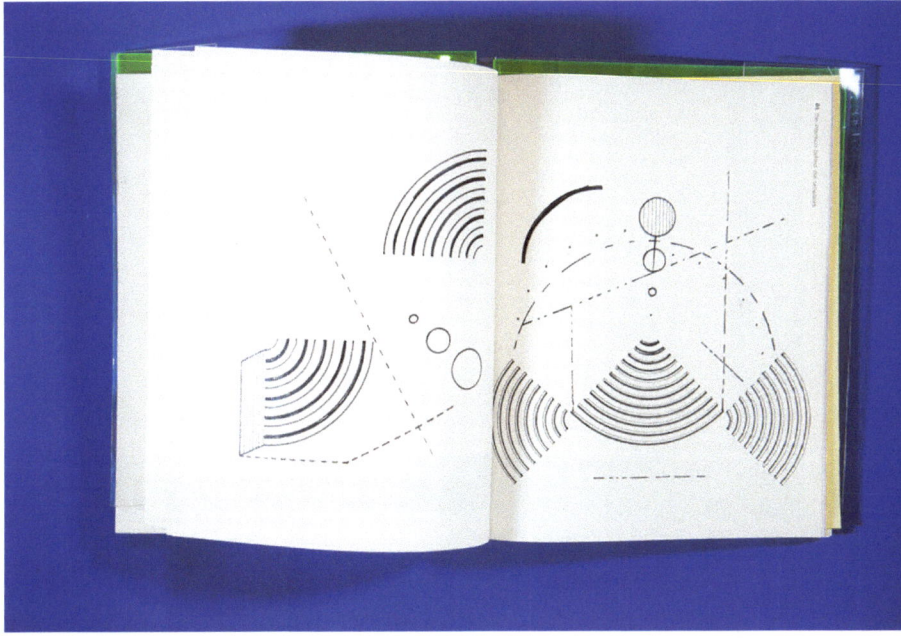

The divergent forms here are all made from the same template.

WHAT YOUR TEACHER IS EXPECTING

Approach divergent thinking with an open mind and to generate ideas without fear about how they connect to a final outcome. Teachers know that you will probably get stuck, and that the key to success in divergent thinking is to keep generating ideas. So even when you think there are no more ideas, just keep making. When you get stuck in divergent thinking you can ask your teacher to help you impose parameters or restrictions on the design exploration, as this can help you focus on generating more ideas.

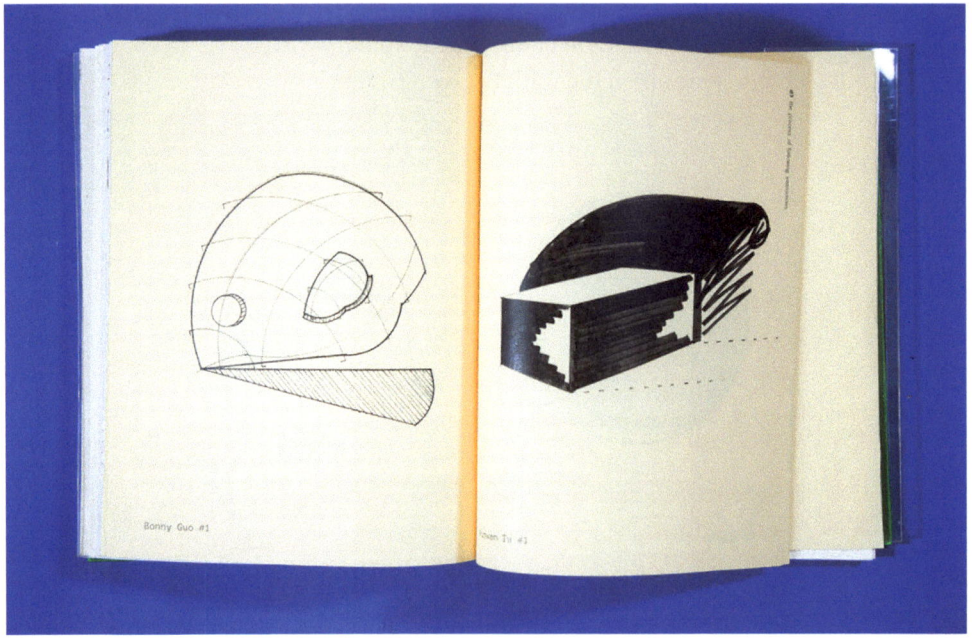

More examples of the divergent forms that are made from the same template.

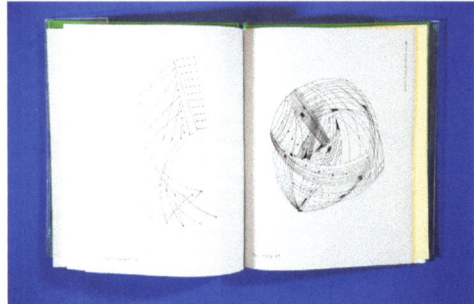

Case study

LOOSE SKETCHES

Loose sketching allows designers to generate many ideas quickly. Loose sketches are not polished, they do not contain a lot of detail but are more like brief notes for ideas.

Title: Animal Logo Design

Level & subject: Intermediate, Branding Design

University: Plymouth College of Art, UK

Teachers: Neil Leonard, James Edgar and Matt Thame

Deliverable: Working files and a PDF presentation that includes the final designs and all sketches, research and process.

PROJECT DESCRIPTION

This undergraduate first year project asks students to design an animal-based logo and visual system for a business. The students draw a client out of a hat, and the emphasis of the project is on generating fresh ideas. The first phase consists of taking notes, drawings and taking/gathering photographs. Idea generation, research and exploration have to be analysed and recorded in a blog and sketchbook. In the second phase, students give a ten-minute pitch of their ideas for approval by their teacher, while a group of classmates acts as a 'client'. The final stage of the project is to present all the work completed for the project. Students must hand in something at each stage, but the brief is not specific about how each part should be presented, so the way the project is delivered can be just as creative as the final artefacts.

Various sketches shown for identity. Student work by Henry Richards.

HOW TO SUCCEED WITH LOOSE SKETCHING

The best mindset for generating ideas, Leonard says, is to be open and inquisitive. 'Students who want to produce one final idea quickly never do as well – they will typically create something entirely generic that doesn't add anything new to what exists in the field.' Sketching and process are important because 'it's rare that a person gets it right the first time, so taking some time to explore a variety of routes will always yield better results'. Leonard points out that in the professional world the entire project would be completed very quickly, perhaps in a day, so the time taken in school is a luxury. Therefore, the time spent generating ideas should always be used wisely to explore, experiment and genuinely learn. Students who spend more time thinking as they draw achieve better results, Leonard explains. While exploring ideas through lots of sketches is good, a student needs to plan to succeed. Leonard points out that while generating lots of ideas is good in this stage, ample time should be left for refinement – not just the night before hand-in!

There is no specific number of sketches; just lots, Leonard says. Although for many students drawing is a pain point. Leonard points out that regardless of sketching skill, 'it is always much quicker to sketch out a few versions of an idea than it is to render them on the computer because the student gets bogged down with details that don't matter at this point'. The advantage of sketching in the process is that if a student has many options they can compare, pick and choose, combine and edit. Leonard warns, however, that students need to be open to rejecting ideas that are not working (no matter how much they like them personally) and they must assess each idea against the requirements of the brief.

Presenting sketches and ideas can be difficult for students and using phrases along the lines of 'I like it' will not persuade a client, nor a teacher, Leonard points out. Each decision should be explained and backed up by some evidence – it also needs to be sold, so Leonard advises that students should be passionate when presenting sketches as this will help the audience believe in the ideas too.

WHAT YOUR TEACHER IS EXPECTING

Aim for lots of sketches, but think your way through ideas – don't just doodle for the sake of presenting a lot of sketches. Use your time wisely – teachers know that the more skills you gain in school learning to sketch and ideate, the quicker you will be able to do so in practice. Don't become attached to your loose sketches. Loose sketches should be critiqued and discussed and discarded. Be open to refine ideas in loose sketch form.

Final identity with comps. Student work by Henry Richards.

Case study

TIGHT SKETCHES

Tight sketches do not have to be beautifully crafted or highly refined but should be accurate enough to show how the elements and composition of the ideas will work. Tight sketches can be done by hand or as very rough drafts in the computer, and will help to refine and communicate your ideas to others.

Title: Design and the Future of Publishing

Level & subject: Intermediate, Publication Design

University: Parsons, The New School, USA

Teachers: Juliette Cezzar

Deliverable: The final design can be a digital or physical publication. The students featured in this case study created a hard-bound book with a foil-stamped cover.

PROJECT DESCRIPTION

In this undergraduate open brief, a communication design BFA student is teamed up with a social research student to create a publication exploring a theme interesting to both. The teams work together using sketches and computer drafts to define an idea before co-creating the final artifact. Content for the publication must be assembled from one (or multiple) sources. The final design must take into account the relationship of form to content, reader to writer, virtual to physical.

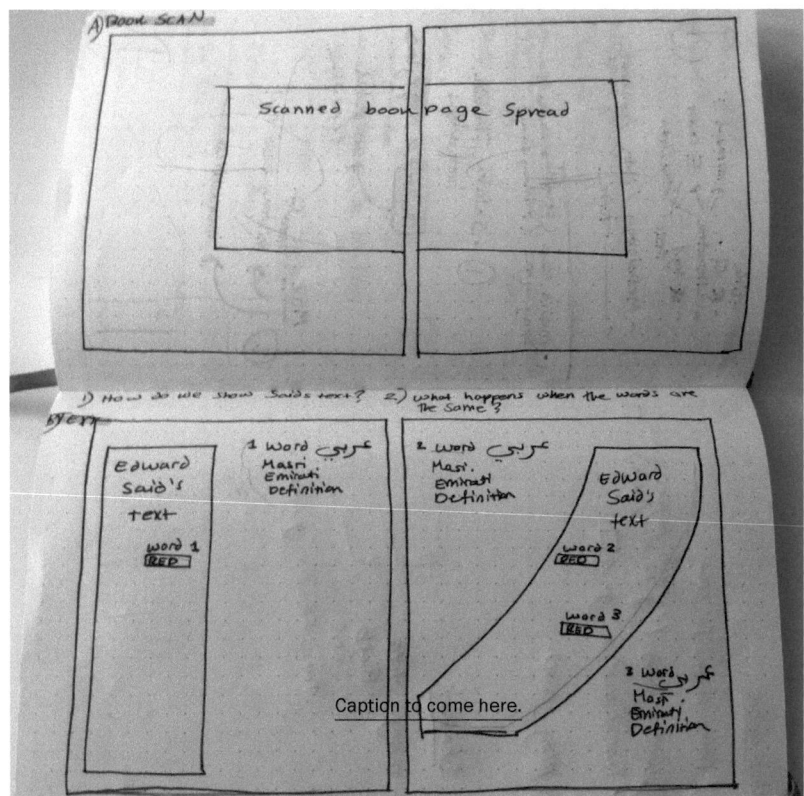

Caption to come here.

HOW TO SUCCEED WITH TIGHT SKETCHES

Juliette says students do better when they approach this work without a picture of the end result in the mind, because 'when they have that picture already, they tend to edit their notes and ideas ahead of time to fit the form they want to make'. Tight sketches flesh out detail, but they are still an exploratory tool, so allow these sketches to lead where they need to go, don't aim for a predetermined end result. This is especially important when working in a team, Cezzar says, 'because different students will have different ideas, or in the case of a non-designer, may not have a picture in the mind at all'.

Cezzar says that during the process of sketching, 'before arriving at the final form, students often start to worry that their ideas aren't good (or unique) enough'. Tight sketches and drafts help students flesh out ideas to see if they will work and if they are interesting enough to pursue.

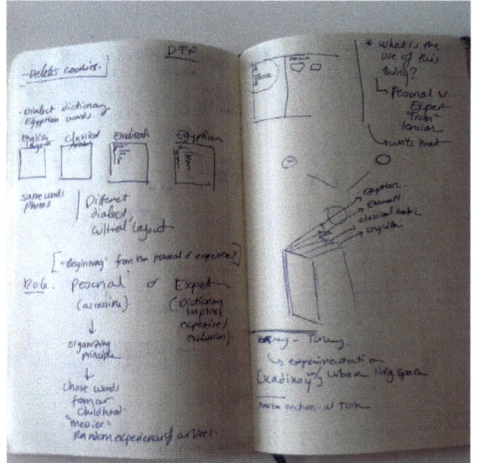

Sketches and notes continue to supply ideas through the design phase of the project.

Computer sketches present in-process ideas.

This screen grab shows the design becoming more refined and exact on the computer.

Using computer drafts as tight sketches can be a good way to present ideas that are not fully formed or in process, as they can be more understandable. The presentation created by two students working on a visual dictionary (pictured opposite) was developed from notes made by hand with pen and paper.

Ideas must be debated, discussed and refined to be useful, Juliette explains, and some feedback from critique is more useful, and some is less useful. By working with tight sketches rather than loose sketches, feedback can be more thoroughly incorporated, tested, and retained or discarded before much time is invested making them perfect in the computer.

After a round of critique and feedback on the computer drafts, the two students created another round of tight hand sketches – the resulting design idea is much more visual and diagrammatic. Notice that the tight sketches shown here are drawn with a purposeful lack of small details in order to communicate the concept without yet committing to a visual form.

——— WHAT YOUR TEACHER IS EXPECTING

Approach tight sketches with the idea that they are still open and imperfect. You should feel less attached to your work at this stage and less worried about the level of finish because they are still not final ideas. The more open to feedback and compromise you are at this stage the more easily tight sketches can be critiqued and discussed and potentially be improved.

See more student examples at: www.bloomsbury.com/the-graphic-design-process-9781350050785

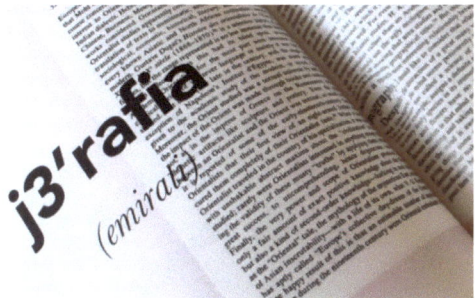

The final bound book design.

CHAPTER THREE

DEVELOP

Once you have generated many ideas and, with the help of your teacher, narrowed them down to the most promising options, you are ready for the process of refinement, which will result in a design direction ready for production (deployment). In the 4D process, refinement falls under the 'Develop' phase. Development can be the most painful, yet satisfying, part of the design process because it is here that you will find out if your design ideas are viable (or can be developed).

The Design and Develop phases of the 4D process tend to blend into each other. If your ideas prove to be weak, you may have to go back to the phase 2: Design and generate new ideas. Similarly, the line between phase 3: Develop and phase 4: Deploy – where refinement ends and production begins – can also be blurry. Efficient decision-making, and time management are crucial to a successful develop phase. This will allow for the best possible design outcome and a healthy mental state for you. Students who are constantly working late nights to try to 'catch up' to meet deadlines end up mentally drained and have work that is less successful.

CONVERGENT THINKING

Convergent thinking is the opposite of divergent thinking in that you are seeking to narrow down, rather than expand, potential design options. In convergent thinking, ideas are whittled down via a process of experimentation, testing and refinement. We experiment by trying numerous different ways of approaching the design idea to see what works and then discard what doesn't. What is kept is then refined by making changes and alterations. During this process, some ideas may even meld together. Each round is shown to the teacher for feedback and the most promising designs are then subjected to more rounds of experimentation and refinement (and possibly user-testing as well). Ideally you will enter the development phase with some ideas, and emerge with one design direction ready for production.

Convergent thinking explores how a design could work. Convergent thinking must also be systematic to get the best results. Thinking of the larger aspects and smaller aspects of the design is crucial, as you must make both large moves and small moves to arrive at good design decisions.

Student Example

Let's look at a student we will call Jessie. Jessie is beginning the development of a website for a project about online data safety and sharing. A wireframe and a journey map for the website has been made and Jessie has completed the design phase of the project through exploration. The visual design now has a general direction and a concept, and they have now developed some initial directions for the site. It is time to make some visual decisions about how the images, colours and typography will actually be composed on the home page.

Jessie posted her submission online and wrote the following for a description of her exploration:

'I tried to work on different colours this week. I will stick to the initial one since the blue refers to the technology and the data, whereas the fuchsia refers to the more human, kind-hearted feel. There are other combinations that I found interesting, but I am not sure they communicate the donation aspect of the project in the same way. I think that the current one opens up for the possibility to add several secondary colours, which makes the colour palette richer.

In terms of typography, I have explored several options. I found Interstate to be very attractive for its simplicity and presence. GT Haptik is also another choice to consider as it is more relevant to the idea of a revolution.'

Three convergent option examples of student work by Maria Bahous.

Jessie's work shows three variations and options for colour, image, layout and type treatments to see what works and what does not. Notice how the same visual information is used on each option, but the treatment of the information changes. Jessie is trying to see how scale, hierarchy, colour, typeface choice, etc work and interact when they are applied differently using the same content. Jessie plays with format and how the use of graphics can be applied to communicate their message in the most engaging and appropriate way. They speak about the decisions being made around colour and what it means conceptually and compositionally.

As with divergent thinking, just doing a lot of versions won't necessarily get the best results. If you work too narrowly, only trying slight variations (say experimenting only with shades of green instead of other colours), you will not be able to fully explore the possibilities of the design. Conversely if you work too broadly, say only producing large variations (like trying blue, green and orange) and do not explore the small variations (like the shades of green) you will not have explored the idea in sufficient detail. Always link back to your concept and audience when making design decisions. There must be a balance of both large and small moves. This diagram visualises a good convergent thinking process.

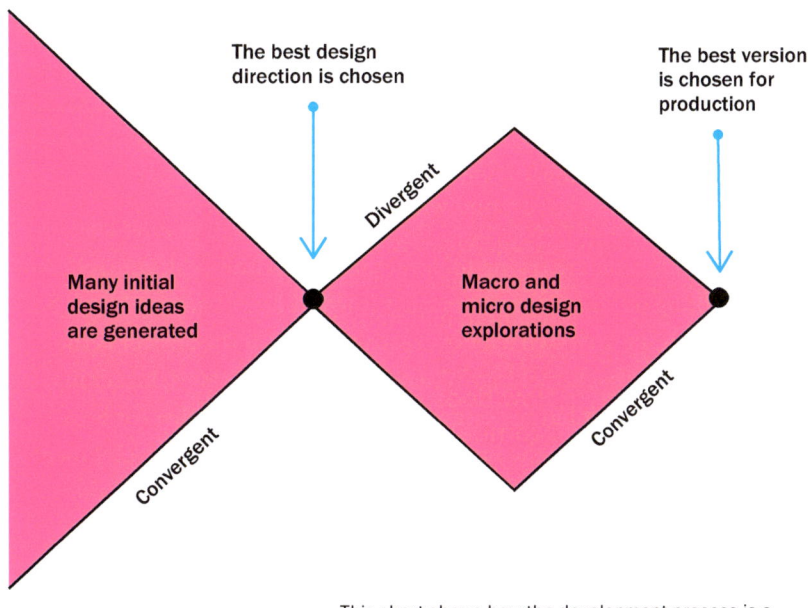

This chart shows how the development process is a series of 'funnels'.

When to keep going and when to go back: Murder your darlings

We can easily waste time in convergent thinking by overworking or decorating (adding design elements that do not add value or alter the design). Some students purposefully avoid making difficult choices, and end up with an unresolved design. When you have several ideas, but the design is not working or is cluttered, sometimes the only way to move the development forward is to 'murder your darlings'. 'Darlings' are the part of a design that we have invested a lot of time and energy into but are actually getting in the way of making a design succeed, so we must 'kill' them.

We talked about the deep freeze technique in the last chapter and while this method can help, it can be harder to apply in the develop phase. The economic theory of 'sunk cost' helps to explain this phenomenon. Sunk cost is when we continue spending money on something that isn't working because we cannot bear to lose the money we already paid out, even though we will lose more money if we continue down the path and the entire investment is lost. We also tend to value things we have, more than things we don't have. In this analogy think of money as your creative effort into the investment (your project). There is a natural tendency to avoid throwing away money/work (effort). We tend to think the ideas we already have are better than any we might get by starting again. It can be hard to tell when we are wandering down an unproductive road and we may wait too long before stopping. Failure in the development stage can often be traced to not recognising you are putting in good money (effort) for a path that is no longer good for your investment (project).

If you have done many versions of the design and it still doesn't work, it may be because you are trying to 'force' an idea. Always ask yourself: Am I still working on this design because it is working, or because I have been working on it (i.e. invested a lot of creative effort)? If the answer is the second, consider backtracking. When a teacher suggests backtracking, this is a very difficult but necessary conversation. No teacher (or boss) wants to waste work. At the same time some of the biggest development successes happen when we ditch work that cannot be developed into a successful outcome. So our advice is to discuss the decision with your teacher first (they may have a way to resolve your issue) and then, if needed, throw it out and start again.

Thinking of design as 'wicked problems' and 'design problem spaces'

Convergent thinking is difficult because there are multiple possible visual solutions to any design project, and the best option to choose isn't always obvious. Design problems have been described as 'wicked'[1] – meaning they are complex and with no clear (visual) solution. This is partly why design school is difficult: because we must wrestle with complex, ill-defined or vague problems that could take any number of possible successful visual forms. Design problems usually have no 'right' answer. Instead there are many 'right' answers, and 'good enough' answers, and the skill of a designer lies in choosing between them all.

One way to help you think through the options and improve your work during convergent thinking is to think of design in terms of problem spaces and problem space solutions. A problem space is all the things that are not working (or not working well) within a design. At any given time, multiple small or large problem spaces in a design can be happening at once.

Here, blue type doesn't work against the background; making it bigger doesn't solve the problem; making it white and small means it is too small to read. But making the type yellow solves the problem space.

---

1 The term 'wicked problems' comes from Richard Buchanan's 1992 paper 'Wicked problems in design thinking'. 'Problem spaces' is an idea from Bryan Lawson's book *How Designers Think* (1993).

Problem spaces can be conceptual too, such as when an image communicates the wrong message. Problem spaces vary, they can be big or small, some are easily seen, others less so, obvious or subtle. A critique is where your teacher and fellow students help point out your problem spaces for you.

When developing a project, you are mostly making a series of moves targeting problem spaces. For example, the design may need more negative space so you might make certain elements smaller in a composition to give more room around them. However, as everything is connected to everything else in design, this means each time you make a move to solve a problem space you will probably create another problem space. Furthering the previous example, that negative space you made by making elements smaller in that composition may now have created a new problem space with legibility due to type being too small. A successful design solution resolves all the problem spaces.

Because solving a problem space will likely create another problem space, you can't just 'follow teacher orders' to succeed. If you just do the changes your teacher suggests to solve a problem space and then ignore, or not try to solve any resulting problem spaces, you may not improve the design and sometimes you might make it worse.

You must try the moves your teacher suggests and then attempt to resolve each new problem space you create. You need to apply your own design understanding to this work. There are times when a teacher's order is very straightforward and should be followed directly. However, most of the time it is best to treat teacher advice as a start, a 'trampoline' to bounce off, not 'marching orders to follow'. Following orders without looking at the results and making additional refinements in this way means although you 'did what your teacher told you to do', your design will not end up not looking very good. This will probably make you frustrated.

Design teachers teach by suggesting problem space solutions and they will try to predicting (as well as they can) what will happen because of the moves they suggest. Therefore design teacher advice come across as vague or uncertain; sometimes teachers just do not know how their advice will work out. Most teachers will acknowledge this uncertainty but some will not. The key to working with teacher feedback in the develop stage is to become comfortable with uncertainty.

SOME PEOPLE LIKE CATS

Sounds crazy to me, but there are definitely some people out there who just don't understand why these people like cats. They don't get why people have them, why many spend countless hours looking at hundreds upon hundreds of pictures of them — and the videos! Why so many viral videos of cats? Not only are these people not cat people — they don't even get cat people.

SOME PEOPLE LIKE CATS

Sounds crazy to me, but there are definitely some people out there who just don't understand why these people like cats. They don't get why people have them, why many spend countless hours looking at hundreds upon hundreds of pictures of them — and the videos! Why so many viral videos of cats? Not only are these people not cat people — they don't even get cat people.

The composition on the left has a problem space: the image of the cat isn't reading as the first thing a viewer would see on the page. A change in the scale of the cat image may fix that problem, but then the poster on the right shows new problem spaces that occur – now there is a cramped space for the title and copy.

Becoming comfortable with uncertainty

The uncertainty presented by both design projects and teachers can be tough to deal with when you first start design school. Throughout our pre-college schooling, we have been trained to expect teachers to be able to tell us exactly what is right (and wrong) with our work. As a result, many college design students expect the same kind of answers from design teachers and are often surprised at how ambiguous and 'vague' design teacher feedback can be. Design teachers are not intentionally vague of course, but as we have pointed out, the creative process itself is uncertain, ambiguous and unpredictable.

Design teachers tend to see uncertainty as possibility, and ambiguity as opportunity in design development. There can sometimes seem to be 'unwritten rules' about what your design teacher expects, and this can be very puzzling at least at first. We have seen as many students get frustrated that their teachers won't 'tell me what to do' as those who complain that their teachers 'keep telling me what to do'. Expecting all the answers from your teacher is understandable, but to succeed you must let go of the idea that there is one clear and certain outcome possible or that your teacher can give to you, because there just isn't.

A common student complaint during the development process is that design teachers seem to work on an 'I'll know it when I see it' way, rather than concretely describing how to get to a solution. This is a good thing; teachers usually don't want to decide what the end result should look like, because they are seeking to help you craft your own ideas into a final project. If your teacher art directs you so closely that you never learn to make decisions or explore yourself then you will not be able to make good design decisions without them around. Fortunately, or unfortunately, your design teacher will not be with you at your desk at your next design job. So, in order to survive without them, one of the things you need to develop to make these design decisions is a 'design eye'.

Developing a design eye

Design is subjective, but good designers tend to develop an appreciation of certain kinds of design aesthetics and choices – they develop what is sometimes called a design eye. A design eye is a kind of taste. Taste is liking certain kinds of things in preference to other kinds of things. Liking is built by looking at things – beautiful and interesting, challenging and ugly – and by talking about what you like (and don't) with other people. One of the things we hope you 'catch' (or internalise) from your design school is the taste of your design teachers.

Subjectivity is a judgement that is not always based on objective facts, but sometimes on opinion, formed by previous influences and experiences. Taste informs your subjectivity. Both taste and subjectivity are hard to learn because they are difficult to explain. Both are a feeling, a part of the designer's intuition, and both help you sort good design choices from

Here, we can see two very different presentations of a hamburger being served. In design, the ability to direct and choose photography with taste can mean the difference between selling the burger and not. Which one of these images shows good design taste? Hint: Which one would you want to eat based on the style of the photo?

not so good design choices. Taste may or may not be addressed in some design schools, but 'having the right taste' does matter because it informs your design choices. All designers have taste and your design teachers are no different.

It is important to acquire the right kind of 'designer's taste'. You can do this by immersing yourself in art and design culture: art films, beautiful books, exhibitions and galleries. In school you are surrounded by teachers with different tastes. Use them as sounding boards and seek their opinions. Find out where they get their design inspiration. Many professional designers collect examples of good design, and this helps build taste as well as providing a tool for creative thinking. Building your taste level will help you become a better designer because the better your taste, the better your design choices will be. During development and convergent thinking you can use your taste to guide your choices.

WORKING WITH YOUR INSTRUCTOR

You learn to design by making design and by talking about what you make. When teachers talk with you about your work it is called a critique. The critique is the primary method of teaching and learning in the design studio, although critique happens in professional practice too. As the name suggests critique has a 'negative' focus, in that it is mostly about what can be improved, rather than what is already working. The idea (and even the name) sounds harsh, and it can be, but if you think about it the method makes sense. While we learn something from knowing what we do right, we learn far more from understanding what we did wrong. Without honest feedback, we will not hear or see what we need to know to improve our work. The critique is particularly intensive and collaborative in the Develop phase, and part of succeeding in this phase, and indeed in design school overall, is learning how to navigate the critique.

Critiquing methods

Teachers sometimes 'group (or 'peer') critique' by gathering students in front of a screen or by looking at printouts on a table or pinned to a wall. Group critique is more common in the Development phase as different perspectives from your peers will assist in convergent thinking – helping you to choose the best ideas. In group critique you are expected to explain your choices and you are sometimes required to 'defend' your work. You and your classmates will be encouraged to contribute ideas as well as criticism, allowing you to all work together like designers do in professional practice – collaborating and helping each other.

During the develop phase teachers will sometimes 'cruise' the classroom, moving from student to student to sit beside them doing a 'one-on-one'.[2] This critique mode is similar to the way junior and senior designers work together in practice. During a one-on-one your teachers will help you to work through design problems by sketching or working with you on the computer. Part of what they are doing is showing you how they approach problems rather than just telling you. By sketching over your work,

---

2 This kind of teaching is often called a 'desk crit'.

 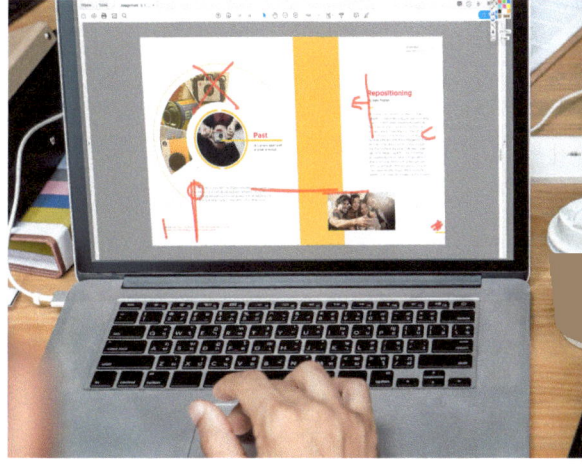

Design teachers often draw over your work, even when they are online.

teachers can show you how they would solve a problem. At the same time they are teaching 'designer code', such as drawing two parallel lines and a squiggly line between them can represent type. This kind of side-by-side teaching helps you understand how to think like a designer, so watch what your teacher does. Ideally your teacher will 'talk aloud' while they work to explain what they are doing, but if they don't, ask questions.

Online critique is automatically one-on-one and at the same time a group critique. Your classmates (should be) able to see your work and what everyone says about it so you can work together. However, students do not always take advantage of group critique online, because it can be tempting to save time by just looking at feedback on your own work. Online students who do this will be missing an important part of a design studio class. You can learn by what your teachers says to others just as much as what they say to you, so be sure to look at and comment on your classmate's work.

When you learn online, take all the opportunities you can to practice giving feedback to your classmates so you learn to talk (and write) like a designer. As you cannot always sit with your teacher working side-by-side online, the critique is inevitably more one-way than it is on-site. This means asking questions is even more important when you are an online student. Especially ask why a teacher is making a suggestion – or what their thought process was – that way you can 'watch' how your teacher solves design problems. Take all the opportunities you can to ask questions about the feedback you get from your teacher.

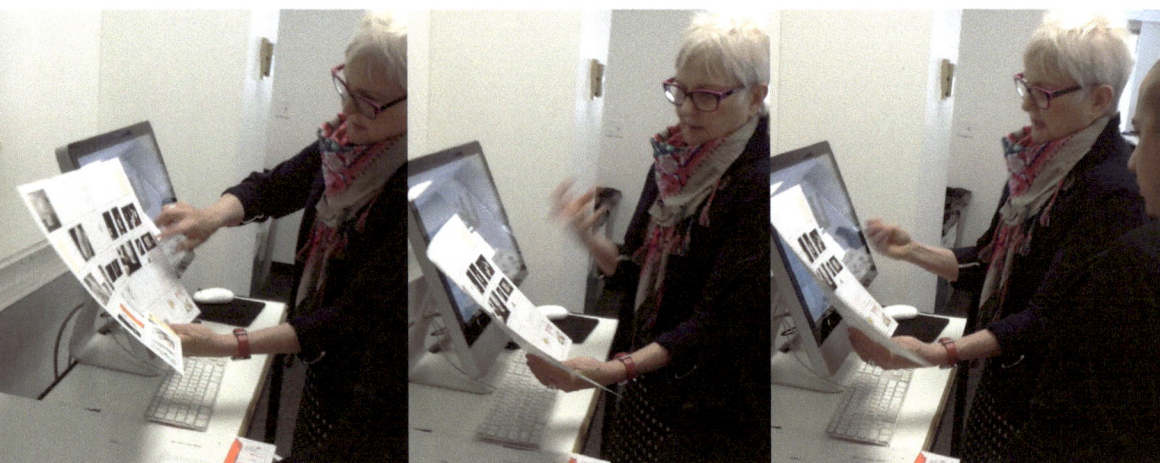

Design teacher Mary makes a 'camera flash' gesture that helps her student understand that 'this needs heft' means 'make it brighter'.

Understanding designer talk

Teachers will sometimes use language in the critique (or in this book) that is confusing. There are unfamiliar technical and professional terms of course, but sometimes design teachers use words that literally don't make sense. You may hear something like 'you need to make this pop' or 'we need a little heft here' or even 'this type is kind of crunchy'. To which you may (reasonably) ask yourself, what does 'pop' mean? How can a design that doesn't weigh anything be 'hefty'? What on earth does 'crunchy' look like? Understand that when your teacher talks this way it is coming directly from their designer's intuition. They are trying to explain concepts that are difficult to put into words, and this language is a kind of shortcut. Compare 'we need to make this pop' with 'there's a problem space here with the contrast, and by laying a brighter colour in this element perhaps we can give it the kind of emphasis it needs to better attract the eye?' The first is a lot quicker! This kind of talk is called an 'aesthetic descriptor' and if you watch designers talking you can see that even their hand gestures synch up and help explain what they mean.

A common student complaint is that the teacher is 'imprecise' or 'vague', and aesthetic descriptors can be part of the reason. While it can be frustrating when you teacher talks this way, designers speak this way in practice too, so you need to learn to interpret and use this kind of talk. Teachers, especially when they are also practicing designers, can be used to talking this way that they forget to explain precisely what they mean, assuming you will figure it out. If this happens ask your teacher to explain further – pretending you understand when you don't doesn't help you.

Subjectivity in the critique

As we spoke about earlier with the 'design eye', design is inevitably subjective because there is no objective right or wrong answer: judging design is, in part, a matter of opinion. A graphic designer's subjectivity is shaped – at least in part – by their professional experience, and this will determine how they respond to a design. So it makes sense then that design teachers will use their subjectivity alongside other more objective criteria when they assess your work.

Part of learning design is learning your teacher's subjectivity, to be able to see as your teacher sees. This ability is called 'professional vision'. Once you acquire professional vision you will be able to analyse design in a way that is different to non-designers. It will become part of your own designer's intuition. Once you learn to see as your design teacher sees, you cannot unlearn it. This shows why picking the right design school is crucial; not only do you need to learn from the strongest designers possible, but every school has its own aesthetic, which will influence and inform your subjectivity.

Perhaps because subjectivity appears entirely personal, rather than connected to experience, students often resist the idea that what their teacher 'likes' is a valid way to assess work. The common student

Design teachers and clients may have subjective opinions based on their own personal likes or dislikes.

complaint 'my teacher just doesn't like my work' is often used as a reason to reject teacher advice because it is opinion. While this is an understandable reaction, and you will probably feel this way at least once during design school, it is a self-defeating course of action. When a teacher 'doesn't like' your work, you do need to try to understand the subjective reasons for their assessment. After all, they are connected to the professional world you seek to enter.

We suggest you try thinking about it this way: Teacher subjectivity comes from experience, and your design teacher can see in a way that you do not (yet). Therefore, teacher advice is always worth listening to even when you disagree with what they like (or dislike), because this helps you understand how your teacher sees. This is a step closer to seeing as they see – to acquiring professional vision – which is important to your development as a designer.

While you should always be open to teacher feedback, as you progress to the senior level it is appropriate to start to argue for your subjective viewpoint as you will have to do this once you leave school. A 'let me show you what I mean' conversation is a more healthy way to work with your teacher than refusing or ignoring their advice. You should only defend an idea when you can prove that it will work, not just because it is your idea. Your teacher is analogous to a client or art director, and their idea will win in the end unless you prove that yours is a truly better. Learning to accept this is part of being a designer, we are after all seeking to be paid creative professionals. While you are in school you are essentially paying to have a teacher's opinion.

Clients have subjectivity too, which can often lead them to make poor decisions. Teachers will tell you if they do not like your work, but clients tend to be politely silent. It is easier to argue for your work with another designer because clients either won't, or do not have the language to describe what is not working. It is your job as a designer to help the client talk about design, and to guide them to the best solution for what the project needs. You can draw upon the way critique is done in design school to help you with this task.

WORKING WITH THE CRITIQUE

Good design critique follows the general pattern we outline in this section. Although of course the content will vary wildly depending on the project.

Characteristics of good critique

Firstly, the teacher should acknowledge your effort and praise if and where appropriate. However, as we have noted, critique in the graphic design studio tends to focus on what isn't working so you cannot expect this to always happen. Effort isn't gradable on its own, and effort is assumed rather than praised. If you thrive on praise this can be difficult to adjust to, but that's good training for the professional world as praise can be small from clients too. Praise usually comes in the form of money in the professional world.

Teacher critique should identify the best design and/or ideas and describe why they are promising, so that you can learn from what you are doing right. Of course, the teacher should also identify weak design and/or ideas and describe why they are not working so that you can learn from where you went wrong. As discussed, teachers will highlight the specific problem spaces within the most promising design(s) and describe why they are problem spaces. They will give you clear advice that can be used to solve any highlighted problem spaces. Teachers may ask questions that don't necessarily require an answer; they are tools for

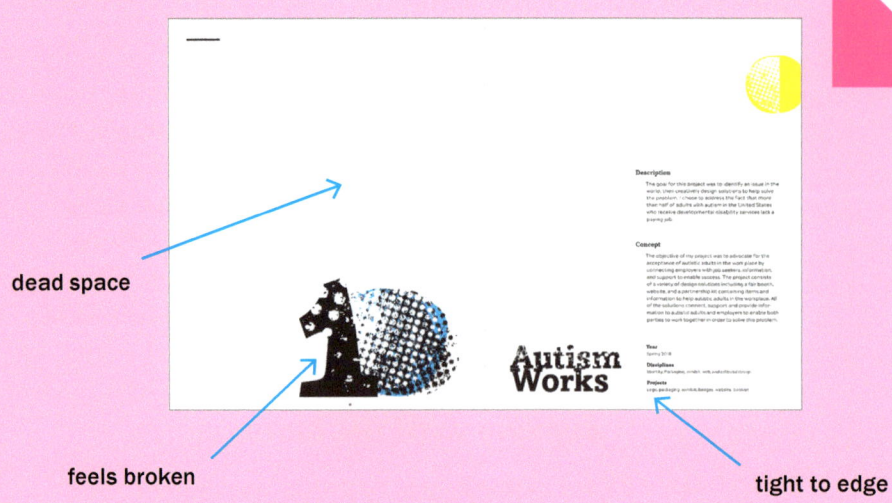

Student Example

The example above shows the call out notes made on a PDF by an online design teacher. The entire note (below) shows that there is a mixture of positive and negative comments, as well as suggestions for improvement. This example demonstrates the way teachers point out problem spaces and ways you can solve them in the critique.

Dead space: Your layout has a lot of open white space which is good. However, the top left page area is "dead space". This area needs to be activated with something. It could be moving the graphic at the bottom into the open space or something else. Scale could be employed with the graphic.

Feels broken: The graphic at the bottom of the page is engaging and I like it, but it feels like the "1" is broken. Your concept is not related to breaking or broken so I would make the letter form more stable feeling. Making it straighter could achieve this effect.

Tight to edge: The content including the type at the bottom of the page is cramped and tight to the edge. It feels awkward and is drawing my eye off the bottom of the page instead of keeping me moving around the composition. You should try moving that copy column and title up a bit to allow a bit more space to breathe.

thinking through the design problem. For example, a teacher may ask you how you can create more negative space in a composition. A question or a series of them might lead you through a set of design choices to a new insight or solution.

Teachers should explain why the suggestion for solving a specific problem space should work so that you can understand and learn from the way your teacher will approach solving design problems. Ideally your teacher will identify potential difficulties with applying their advice, and suggest alternative solutions (if possible) and illustrate this advice with a visual example (if appropriate). Finally, design teachers usually solicit questions so that you can participate in a dialog. Hopefully the critique will end on a positive note. However, if you have not done the work you have been asked to do or have supplied substandard work, do not expect a lot of positivity. Design learning is difficult learning so this can be very important, especially in the Develop phase.

Peer critique

In the design studio online or on-site, you will be called upon to give critique to your peers. This is because the ability to clearly and succinctly inform others about what is and is not successful in their design, concept, and execution, is part of working with others. No one gets to a senior design position without developing this ability. Using the same structure as your teacher uses is a good place to start. There is always something that can be improved or refined in any design. It is important to point out if the project was successful, but also what was unsuccessful and what could be improved. Otherwise, you are not helping and nobody will get better.

A successful critique should speak to the quality of the design, the formal execution and the concept of the assignment you are reviewing, try describing:

Successful critique includes >>

- what works and why

- what didn't work and how you would improve it

- anything you learned from looking at the work

- any ideas that you thought might be useful.

Always consider the formal elements and principles of design: colour, typography, composition, image use, concept, etc. You can also comment on how your classmate did or did not follow directions and of course the overall quality and impact of design. When looking critically at the work of your fellow students also think about your own concepts and ideas; often finding problems in other designers' work can help you to identify issues in your own work.

Participation

As a design student you get to both observe and participate in other students' learning during the critique. Through your assignments, you get a series of opportunities to talk about design with a group. Learning in a group is easier than learning by yourself because we learn in part by watching what others do and what they are told to do. In the design studio classroom you get to practice and improve your ability to critique by listening to your teacher and your fellow students. In a critique, listen carefully to what others are being told – especially if the critique is around failure of some kind. Most likely this information applies to your own work and is meant for you just as much as the person presenting.

As a secret tip, actively buddy up to the best students in the class and ask for their help. Design learning is partly a process of being immersed in a group. Not only does getting help from your classmates help your grades, it also helps emotionally. Learning design is difficult, it's uncertain and any company and support will be helpful. If you are an online student this advice applies doubly so. In fact online learning makes it easier, you can form social media groups to solicit advice while you work on projects.

Reframing the critique

Part of giving and taking critique is learning not take it personally, and this can be very difficult. No matter how pleasant an individual teacher might be, honest design feedback hurts feelings sometimes. Critique is not about you, it is just about your work, and it can be very hard to separate yourself from your work. However, separate you must or you will be a very unhappy designer. Critique in design school is a training ground for how to deal with this unavoidable and sometimes unpleasant part of being a graphic designer. Like a boot camp, you are exposed to a gruelling training regimen that eventually toughens you up. You may think that receiving a negative critique from a teacher might be as bad as it gets, but some of the worst critiques are from silent, polite clients. That kind of critique can be job threatening.

It is surprising how many beginning design students expect validation rather than criticism, and how many students are apt to blame their teacher and complain that they are mean, or believe critique is used to get them to quit school. The opposite is the case; teachers are judged on successful students and good student work. Keep in mind that the goal of the critique is the same for you and your teacher: to improve your work.

No one likes to hear that their work doesn't measure up so there may be negative emotions and that is understandable. We advise you to walk into every critique assuming that at least some aspects of your work will need to be improved. This is not a negative mindset, but rather a 'learner' mindset, meaning you are primed and ready to hear advice for improvement. Our second piece of advice is to lose the fear that you can't think of more ideas. Part of what makes critique a problem is when you think that your best ideas have been shot down and there's nothing left. Strive to treat your design ideas like candies in a bag. If a candy falls on the ground and gets dirty, throw that candy away, pick out another candy from the bag and see how it tastes.

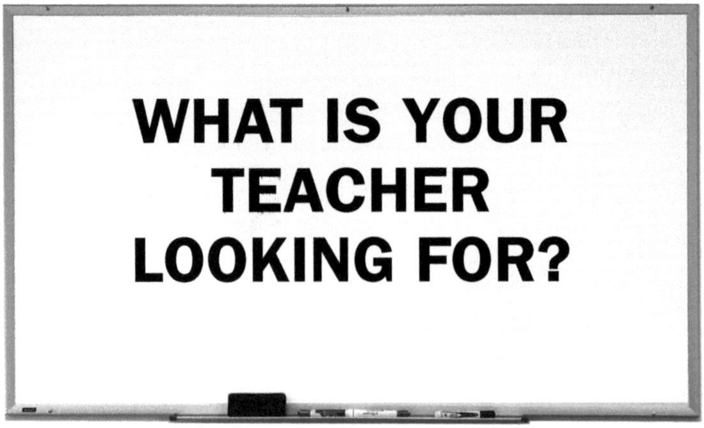

WHAT IS YOUR TEACHER LOOKING FOR?

In the following pages we include specific examples of student projects and what can be learned while working with your teacher during the Development phase.

- Asking questions
- Subjectivity
- Critique
- Group critique

Case study

ASKING QUESTIONS

Questions from teachers during the critique don't necessarily have to be answered but can instead be used as tools for thinking.

Title: Identity Systems Project

Level & subject: Advanced, Branding Design

University: North Carolina State University, USA

Teacher: Denise Gonzales Crisp

Deliverable: Logo and secondary marks with associated graphic elements, typefaces and a colour palette and a system of applications, which includes a business system and a style manual.

―――― PROJECT DESCRIPTION

For this project, students create a graphic identity system by choosing a company or institution and writing a design brief. The students design an identity and create physical and digital touchpoint prototypes that may include marketing collateral products, packaging, interior signage and the like.

―――― HOW TO SUCCEED BY USING TEACHER QUESTIONS

Even a very simple question can give you a new perspective to help you to think through your work, as the student project shown in this shorter case study illustrates. Here, Denise's student began by writing a brief describing an organization putting on an event

 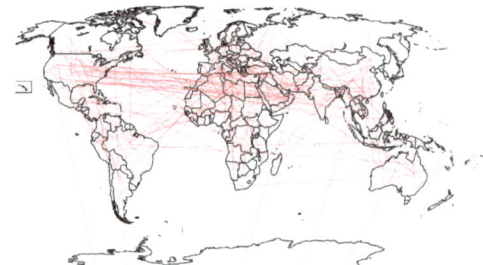

Static map graphic.

called 'Breaking down Barriers', then she decided on a theme of 'connections' for the design. However, the graphic system originally featured a generic and static Decatur map (above left).

Denise asked the student that if the event was designed to 'challenge territorial identities and to ask people to reconsider their perspectives about traditional boundaries, why are you using such a status quo map?' At the heart of this question is a focus on how the visual design might better reflect the keywords of 'challenge' and 'connections'. The student generated a map diagramming the connections using red lines, which becomes the basis of the visual system.

Students are not always expected to answer teacher questions during the critique, but instead use them to think about the work. Here, Denise's simple question lead the student to redesign the wall graphic as three 'interpreted' maps to replace the single ordinary map, and to develop an identity system that better reflected the idea of challenging traditional borders.

Interactive map graphic. Student work by: Kaanchee Gandhi.

Final exhibition design. Student work by: Kaanchee Gandhi.

The final environmental graphic is far more interactive, allowing participants to interact and contribute images, marks, statements and to link the event together. The connecting lines become decorative elements that can even be used on the floor (see above). If the student had chosen to answer the question by defending the original static design, instead of taking on board and thinking about the implications of what Denise asked, the final design would not have been as successful.

────── WHAT YOUR TEACHER IS EXPECTING

Don't automatically respond to teacher questions by defending your work. Pondering and responding to questions teachers pose during the critique can lead your design in a more interesting direction, so be alert to teacher questions and take full advantage of them.

Case study

SUBJECTIVITY

Subjectivity is a personal viewpoint about what is and isn't good design. Teachers use their subjectivity, which is based on their professional experience, to critique your work. Aesthetic choices are in part guided by personal subjectivity.

Title: Hauntology 2.0: Back to the Future Project

Level & subject: First Year Masters, Graphic Design

University: California Institute of the Arts, USA

Teacher: Yasmin Khan

Deliverable: The end product is up to the student, and although it is speculative in nature it must have (and is assessed by) its own well-considered internal logic. For the project featured in this case study, the student envisioned a future where the environment has collapsed, and scientists have developed a synthetic food alternative which can be absorbed through the skin. The task the student set for themselves was to design the 'food' as both a skin decoration and as nutrition. These food images would then be incorporated into a book. The student decided that an appropriate style for the project would be a 'hyperreal' aesthetic inspired by K-pop music videos.

The first round of the student's project did not successfully integrate the "hyper real" style the student was aiming for. Student work by: JunKi Hong.

——— PROJECT DESCRIPTION

This open brief is an exercise in bridging the theoretical with the practical and material, and the work produced is experimental and speculative. Students are asked to create a piece of media designed to communicate with, contact or conjure either the 'dead'/undead (retro-futurist) or future living (future-positivist) people.

——— HOW TO WORK WITH SUBJECTIVITY

As this case study illustrates, aesthetic choices are often guided by your teacher, even if they don't necessarily 'like' the style you have chosen. After a few rounds of developing the visuals for the 'food', Jun (the student) got stuck. Yasmin was not necessarily a fan of the aesthetic he was using but could see that Jun had yet to develop a visual language that embraced and celebrated the hyperreal and synthetic. Instead of telling him to abandon the idea, Yasmin suggested rewatching the videos that were the original inspiration for the project, while the class discussed them and wrote notes. Making notes is a technique that breaks down an aesthetic, style or individual design into words. Explaining or breaking down what makes a design, or a style like the K-pop 'hyperreal' aesthetic, work in words helps you to understand exactly how it works. Once the student understood how this design or a style worked and broke it down into its elements, it was easier to apply to their own work.

The final of the students project more successfully uses the "hyper real" style. Student work by: JunKi Hong.

In the end the project was successful. The images (see above) now look like real food – beautiful yet creepy – which embodies the hyperreal aesthetic she was aiming for (and which the project will be judged by).

Yasmin says that she uses her own subjectivity to help students discard ideas but does not guide students away from any ideas during development. Instead she positions subjectivity as something to be questioned: 'My first response is to question my own values and ask myself why I believe an idea may be weak, if this is really true, or if I'm being prejudiced by my own biases and values.' Yasmin suggests that by adopting this mindset of inquiry as opposed to problem-solving, both students and teachers can remain open to unforeseen outcomes.

──── WHAT YOUR TEACHER IS EXPECTING

Be open to your teacher's subjectivity as it will help you make better design choices. Understand that your teacher uses their subjectivity to assess your work and to give you advice, but they do not solely judge your work by the design they personally do or do not like.

Case study

CRITIQUE

Critique is the primary method of teaching and learning in the graphic design studio. Good critique should be action oriented, concrete and understandable. Design teachers tend to focus on what needs to be improved rather than what is already working

Title: Historical Fiction

Level & subject: First Year Masters, Visual Literacy

University: CalArts, USA

Teacher: Michael Worthington

Deliverable: Book cover that includes front, back and spine. The format for the cover is variable and decided by each student.

PROJECT DESCRIPTION

This project is in two parts. Students first research an art/design movement from a list provided, then use the colour, shapes, motifs, composition and type choices from that movement to make a non-pictorial (abstract) book cover. In a second phase, students choose an interesting, and not necessarily obvious, work of fiction that connects to the art/design style. The choice of book title should have an interesting, and not necessarily obvious, connection with the art/design style. The goal of the project is to understand and be able to work with the components, elements and motifs of a historical style, and to be able to reinterpret or reference that style in a different context. There is a lot of critique and discussion at every stage of the development process.

Final of the book cover project which uses an art movement as inspiration. Student work by: Tracy Thanh Tran.

HOW TO SUCCESSFULLY USE THE CRITIQUE

Good design advice is constructive, identifying problem spaces and potential solutions, as this example of Michael's critique demonstrates:

> 'The form and concept mesh together in innovative ways, there is an interesting dialogue between the Constructivist forms and those forms representative of the text, 1984. This intersection hints at issues to do with government surveillance and spying, false utopia, political oppression, and the possibility that omnipresent media is watching you. The scale of the camera and the eye dominate, as opposed to "the people" who are the nameless masses. Of particular interest is the secondary visual narratives: the camera lens as an eye, the camera as coffin, and the camera poles as prison bars. *Diagonal direction in the composition becomes very important to keep the viewer's eye moving...agitated...* The simple colour palette relates to Constructivism, and though the heavy grey feels appropriately oppressive, it makes the composition feel flat. *There was some discussion as to whether the typeface references Constructivism or American football, and if it is both, is that good? The back cover feels too passive, we asked what could be a counterpoint or additional idea for the back.*'

A series of questions like the ones at the end of the critique are targeted at helping the student through potential next steps. Notice how Michael switches perspective from himself, to the audience, and back again. Teachers often do this to give a 360-degree perspective on your work.

Finals of the book cover project which uses an art movement as inspiration. Student work by: Ella Gold.

Michael says: 'Critique is subjective, but it encourages students to back up subjective comments with objective evidence'. This is good advice and Michael demonstrates how it works this way: 'You can't just say "I don't like that typeface, it doesn't work". That is entirely subjective and helps no one. But if you can say "That typeface doesn't work because it connotes Art Deco and not Constructivism" then you are providing a more concrete (and helpful) statement.'

Michael observes that critique is a process, a way of checking what works and what doesn't, which is like beta testing a product. While critique can point out a problem neither the critique (nor the teacher) should provide the solution. It is up to you to creatively respond to feedback rather than expect an answer to the problem. Pointing out the negative is a way of figuring out what needs fixing, whereas pointing out the positive is just acknowledging what might not need to change. To improve, seek 'negative advice' on your work, as it will be more useful.

Michael points out that teachers sometimes tell students when something is failing, to help them 'see' that failure and not repeat it. But that critique should never be personal: the student and the student's work are two different things – a harsh critique of the work is not necessarily a harsh critique of your personality! It's crucial to separate yourself from your work, this helps you to not take critique personally.

WHAT YOUR TEACHER IS EXPECTING

Critique is subjective but should always be presented in a constructive objective way. Do not just say you 'do not like' something; you should always be able to supply a reason backed up by evidence. Understand that teacher critique is not intended to tear you or your ideas down – they help you make design choices, and improve your work.

Final of the book cover that uses Constructivism as a basis of the book cover design. Student work by: Tracy Thanh Tran.

Case study

GROUP CRITIQUE

Group critique is the method of pinning/showing design work on a wall or screen and discussing it with your classmates. You may be called upon to comment and to explain your design choices.

Title: Type of Music

Level & subject: First Year Undergraduate, Typography

University: UCLA, USA

Teacher: Willem Henri Lucas

Deliverable: The final is 40 CD covers presented as a hardback book.

—— PROJECT DESCRIPTION

This is a tight brief where the focus is on the creative process and the final product is experimental, yet polished. Students choose a favourite song from their favourite artist and create a series of CD covers. The lyrics, song titles, band name and other found and written text and references are used for content. Students design eight sets of five designs each to defined parameters, playing with composition, leading, letter spacing, upper and lower case, etc. In this project students use and learn InDesign and its typesetting tools.

—— HOW TO SUCCESSFULLY USE THE GROUP CRITIQUE

This case study powerfully demonstrates how you can learn both from, and with, your classmates in the design studio. Willem divides the student into groups of five, and each student must put five ideas up on the wall. Everyone in the group must chime in on

Student work by Bethany Rennard.

critique. Lucas says this makes the process more democratic and less scary. Keep this in mind during critique – it is a chance to contribute, not just a source of anxiety.

During group critiques Lucas encourages students to 'read' what the design is about and what the designer's aim could be. Reading is a kind of design analysis, and building this ability gives you stronger critiquing skills. Willem explains that talking about each example gives you an understanding of how communication works – putting analysis into words helps you to better understand how design works. As Willem points out: 'Students need to learn how to talk about design, how to look at it, and translate form back to idea, and idea into the right form. The moment they master that tool, critique becomes an enriching thing, and will not be painful.'

Students in each group work together. They can swap and redo designs, and through group discussion the designs that marry concept and execution the best designs are determined by a majority rules method. Relying on your peers as well as your teacher will help your work become stronger, it follows that you should look to the strongest designers in the class to help you the most. It must be said this technique only works if each student critically evaluates work rather than being personally supportive – so strive to be kind but honest during the critique.

Willem emphasizes that you should gain experience and knowledge during multiple design rounds, each refinement should be better than the one before. This means your teacher should have less to say about your work as the project progresses. If this is not happening, you could try forming your own study group to help you make better design decisions.

WHAT YOUR TEACHER IS EXPECTING

Many heads are better than one when it comes to working through the convergent thinking process. You can form your own study groups to help each other through the design process.

See student examples and read each brief in its entirety at:
www.bloomsbury.com/the-graphic-design-process-9781350050785

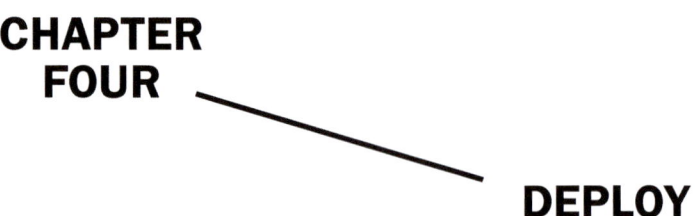

Here we are at the final phase of the 4D design process: Deploy. The focus is now on the production of physical or digital comps and presenting your work. This is where all the fine details are checked and the work is polished. Details matter; spellchecking, image quality, making sure every link is live, checking every pixel, and leaving nothing to chance is the key to success.

In this phase your teacher may suddenly seem extremely picky and ask for you to repeatedly rework copy setting, image quality, written content, paper selection, missing links, etc. This is because getting the details perfect is the sign of a well-trained designer, and what your teacher is doing is putting your work through 'the detail filter' in an effort to train you to get everything right. It is vital to get everything correct because mistakes can be costly, and in the professional world they can even be job ending. The professional world is full of stories of designers sending off work to go live or be printed and later finding issues that turn out to be so costly that the entire project becomes a financial loss. As a result, for better or worse, designers tend to develop a bit of an obsession with getting the details right. Design school is where you should develop a perfectionist mentality because it can take surprisingly large amounts of time and focused attention to address all of the details.

Professionally the deploy phase is when printing and production happens, and/or when coding and development is completed, and a

Sometimes an error is difficult to spot, even in a title.

project goes live. In design school, of course, students (mostly) produce their own work, so there is less teamwork and contact with vendors. However, students do usually give a final presentation to the class and teacher just as a professional designer will give a presentation to get a 'sign off' from a client. Students receive a grade rather than a client 'sign off', so we will talk a little bit about that in this chapter. As we pointed out at the start of the book, talking about your work can be as important as the work itself. In this chapter we will talk about how to make effective presentations.

Our goal for this chapter is to help you to understand the demands of finishing and presenting your work correctly. We will help you to understand the correct amount of time and effort to put into the end of the project. Time and attention to the quality of your deployment work will pay dividends both in school and in the professional world.

PRESENTING YOUR WORK

Most design projects end in a presentation. Professionally a presentation is given to clients (and any stakeholders) with the purpose of getting the work signed off before final production begins. In design school, production has usually been completed so the final design artefacts are shown and talked about, so your presentation is basically a final critique as well as your chance to practice how you speak about design in front of other people.

Talking about your work

Great design should speak for itself, but only after it is out in the world. Before a client will say yes, or you receive a passing grade from your design teacher, you usually have to make a presentation. This means talking in combination with showing your work. In both the professional and the school setting, what you say, and the way work is shown must engage the teacher, clients or stakeholders and leave them feeling confident that the original design problem has been solved.

Presentations have power, and this is something that can take time to understand. Every design teacher has seen mediocre work appear better through a great presentation, or a project appear much worse through a poor presentation. In design school the presentation of your work can directly affect the final grade. It is important to understand what type of presentation is required, and to craft a presentation that will meet that criteria. Here are some key questions you need to consider to properly understand the criteria and the context of a final presentation:

How long should the presentation be? A good presentation is only as long as it has to be. Presentations that go on too long are not helpful and you will often lose the audience's attention. This means you should only include content that is asked for, or is extremely relevant to, the understanding of the final design solution. Sometimes your teacher will provide a time limit. If they do not it is helpful to ask approximately how long your presentation should be.

Who do I need to convince? Knowing who will be at your presentation can help you decide what to include and how to present your work. If the presentation is to the teacher and students in your class, then they have already

<u>Criteria and context for presentation</u>
<<

A student presents work in progress to design teacher Mary Scott.

seen every step of the development. You will not need to present as much background information or project description. Teachers will often bring in people from outside the school (usually other designers) to see final presentations. Try to find out who they are and how much they know about the project before the presentation. You can then craft (or adjust) the presentation to include content that will be relevant and engaging for that audience.

What needs to be covered and what does not need to be covered? After you have established the audience for your presentation you need to think about what specifically needs to be shown, and what should not be shown. If your teacher does not provide a specific list of things to be presented for final evaluation, then ask for clarification. Regardless, be sure that you have completed the work that is expected of you. There is nothing worse than finding out during the presentation that you are missing key parts of the design. For this reason, it can be helpful to establish a checklist based on the original brief, and mark things off as you complete them.

What is the best format for presentation? Some teachers leave the format open for students to choose how they wish to approach the presentation. Other projects are very prescribed and state the correct format to present the work. If the format is up to you to determine, then think about what might be the most effective way to show off your work. Do you need visual aids like slides or infographics? Do you need to be 'in costume'? Do you need to craft a mock-up of a physical item? Do you need to have a website or video cued up and ready to be shown on screen?

Sweating the details

You should consider your presentation as a part of your final project and craft it just as carefully. Misspellings, poorly crafted text and sloppy craftsmanship are all going to impact negatively on your overall evaluation and will usually be reflected in your final grade.

Everyone has given at least one poor presentation. As teachers, we have seen a range of student presentations succeed and fail. The best way to show you how to avoid failing is by using story. The following is a fictitious account based on many of the real-life issues we have seen happen in weak student presentations.

Student Example

In our student story, Chris is giving a final presentation for a class project which includes a variety of physical and digital artefacts:

Chris frantically dashes from the parking lot to class and is late into the room – everyone is already seated and waiting for the presentation to start. Throwing the printed work on a table, Chris rummages around for a flash drive and an adaptor to run the PDF presentation, then darts frantically around the room arranging mock-ups on a table and plugging in computer equipment. While rushing around, Chris constantly apologizes for the smell of the glue barely holding the packaging comp together (it has not yet dried and is causing a strong odour in the room.) Chris also apologizes for the brochure (which is a bunch of loose, untrimmed, pages) explaining that it was not possible to finish the comping because the X-Acto blades ran out late the night before. After pulling up a web browser, Chris realizes there is no Internet connection in the room, which means the homepage cannot be launched. Instead of showing a live website, Chris is instead forced to pull a series of Photoshop files up on-screen and show the site in a static format. Clicking on the homepage layer of the file, Chris turns to the audience and smiles – finally ready to begin the presentation. It is only then Chris notices the shocked crowd of faces staring wide-eyed at the screen that shows the project title headline in bold sans serif type: Presision in Design.

Now let's examine what happened to Chris to see what we can learn about what things we should pay special attention to when preparing to give a presentation.

'Chris frantically dashes from the parking lot to class and is late into the room.' The audience's initial impression is of someone who has trouble meeting basic deadlines. *We can learn from this that you are the first impression.* Being in the room at the right time with your work ready to go (both on-screen and physically on the table) is a big deal. Being on time allows both you and your audience to feel confident about your abilities going into the presentation. We recommend you getting to the presentation early – any rushing around should be finished before the audience ever sees you.

'Chris starts by rummaging for a flash drive and the adaptor to run the PDF presentation, then darts frantically around the room arranging physical materials.' *It is best to be ready beforehand so your setup is minimal.* Your goal is to spend your time addressing the audience at the beginning of the presentation, rather than plugging in and pulling out equipment and materials. Make a list of all the things you will need, and check against this when you are packing to go. Check that your digital files are cued up, and Wi-Fi connections and power cords are ready and set up to go. If you can access the room early go in and set up before your presentation.

'Chris constantly apologizes for the smell of the glue and could not comp a brochure because the X-Acto blades ran out late the night before.' *Plan to complete your work with enough time to allow things to settle, dry, digitally load or be crafted well before your presentation.* Order supplies in advance and keep your eye on things like the levels in your ink cartridges so you do not unexpectedly run out.

'Instead of showing a live website, Chris is forced to pull a series of Photoshop files up on-screen and show the site in a static format.' *Always present in the appropriate format, and plan for any technological issues.* Using a format other than appropriate or required is an obvious problem to be avoided. Have multiple backup options for presentation. For instance, if you have to rely on an Internet connection to show something interactive or moving, be sure you have an alternate presentation like a screen capture recording to show it the way it is meant to be experienced.

'Right when the presentation starts Chris notices the shocked crowd of faces staring wide-eyed at the screen, which is showing the project title headline completely misspelled.' *A presentation with misspellings or grammatical mistakes shows a lack of attention to detail.* Your audience will think that you have not even taken the time and effort to use spellcheck or read your own content. Why should they then expect you to have the attention to detail and organization to make a great project? Spellcheck is free, don't forget to run it right at the end. Don't ignore the titles either, you would be surprised how often it's the large type that is wrong. Don't just spellcheck, make sure you 'sanity check' for correctly spelled but incorrect words and incorrectly phrased sentences. If you are not a native language speaker, find a native speaker to help you.

Finally, this story shows that being in a presentation can make anyone anxious to some degree. *Practising by going through what you want to show and say will always help make a presentation smoother and less stressful.* Set a personal deadline for yourself well in advance of your presentation and give a test presentation to a friend, co-worker (or even your pet). Video and screen capture technologies allows you to record a presentation to check timing and pacing all by yourself in the privacy of your own room so you can feel free to make mistakes without anyone ever knowing.

Explain your work in terms of the design problem to be solved

Once you understand the context and figure out the logistics for your presentation, you will then need to put together a presentation that connects the work you made to the design problem you were given to solve. The best way to do this is to describe the design decisions you made and how they directly connect to solving the design problem. Strive to make the presentation seem like a cause and effect scenario. Talk specifically about what you were asked to do, then connect that to what you did with the design. Refer back to the brief you were given (or wrote) in the beginning of the project to identify the specific challenges.

If you were working from a tight brief, you were most likely given clear and specific criteria for what to do. For example, if you were asked to create a composition that employs scale, in your presentation you would speak specifically about how scale is addressed in your work. Refer directly to any terminology and/or ideas in the brief (and if applicable, information from class lectures and demonstrations). This is your chance to show you have absorbed and can use professional terminology to speak about your design work.

In a presentation where the brief was loose, it is up to you to identify the design problem, and consequently what criteria you should be judged upon. Use plain direct language to explain the criteria, and how your work is a response to the design problem as you identified it. A presentation is not a murder mystery, even the most sophisticated design concepts can be explained in an easily understandable way, using obtuse phrases or overly complicated words does not add value. Direct and clear language in the presentation can still be engaging and interesting. For example, let's pretend that in the Discover phase research determined that your audience would respond to messages printed on large wall-sized graphics pasted in public transit spaces. In your presentation you could then say something clear and direct like 'through research I identified that large transit graphics would be the best way to present messages to this audience'. You would not say something complicated like, 'a mixed methods study design revealed that the target audience would be open to over-scaled environmental ephemera placed in publicly accessible through-spaces'.

Explaining process:
Storytelling and narrative techniques

One way to keep your audience engaged is by crafting a story, which designers often call a 'narrative'. Research shows that humans pay attention to, and like stories, so tell the audience one about your work by presenting an account of connected events relevant to the design problem and solutions. We are designers, not writers, so any narrative should be comprised of visuals accompanied by words that support and fill in the details, not a lot of words with a few visuals thrown in.

A narrative is comprised of parts and your job as a presenter is to decide which parts to include and then arrange them in a way that the audience will care about and pay attention to. Aristotle wrote that a play (narrative) is basically split into two parts: complication and unravelling. To translate this idea to a design presentation, you have two parts: the problem that was given to you (or the one you created for yourself) and then how you solved that problem through design process. Thinking of the story of your work in terms of 'complication' and 'unravelling' adds interest. So ask yourself: What was the problem? What insights did I find? How did I end up solving the problem? Then present the solution as a journey showing how these things were put together to reach the solution.

Presenting your work can be a bit like a dramatic performance. You have an audience who is giving you their time, so you should reward them with an engaging experience. An engaging narrative can start with what is called an 'exposition'. An exposition inserts important information and can consist of:

- dialogue

- background details

- unexpected media

- a backstory

An exposition may consist of <<

Depending on what your presentation needs, including one or more of these things can be a powerful way to begin a presentation.

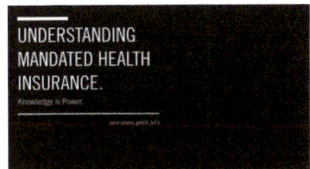  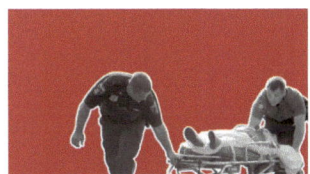
 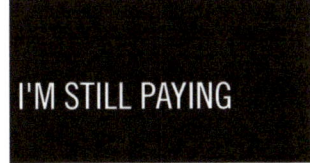 
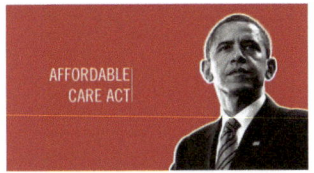  

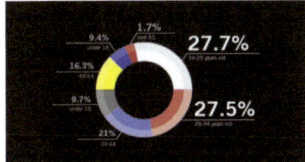  
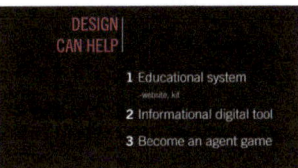 

Student example of narrative presentation. Screen-capture images from original student video by Sami Lukens.

Student Example

Let's look at the beginning of an actual student presentation. We will call the student Pat. Pat has been working on a project around promoting health insurance for college students, and the resulting presentation uses all the exposition ideas we mentioned previously:

Pat begins the presentation by playing a video. The video features Pat riding on the back of a jet ski, on a lake, going fast, smiling and having a great time. But suddenly, the video shows the jet ski ramming into a tree stump on a shore. The video abruptly ends with static on the screen and the camera angle turning over and over as the crash occurs. Pat stops the video and turns to the audience of college students and teachers and asks a question: 'How many of you have health insurance?' After seeing a show of hands from the audience, Pat continues, 'I was in this accident and I did not have health insurance. I am still paying off my medical bills from this accident to this day.' Pat then pulls up a series of charts and graphs showing how few college-age students have health insurance and the monetary ramifications that can happen as a result.

Let's analyse the different aspects of the exposition in Pat's presentation and see what we can learn.

Pat engages in dialogue by asking the audience who has health care coverage. *You can start a presentation by engaging the audience with a question.* Questions can challenge the audience's understanding of the problem and focus them on your topic by making them wonder where you are going with the presentation.

Pat used a series of statistics that showed how serious the lack of health care was in young adults. *Providing background details, such as insights or facts about the project topic, can be a way of connecting the audience to the presentation as well as setting the stage for what is to come.*

Pat used an impactful personal video, which was unexpected media, to illustrate the point that even young people get hurt and need medical assistance. Just because you are presenting your design deliverables in a certain format does not mean you cannot incorporate other forms of media in your presentation. *Switching media, or using unexpected media types, or even just an unexpected image, can both make an impact and set your presentation apart from others.*

Pat told a personal backstory that demonstrated how Pat was previously part of the audience for the project. *Providing a story connected to the project topic can connect either you or other members of the audience to the topic.* If you can connect yourself in a powerful way through a backstory you will speak with more authority as well as making the audience more interested in the rest of your presentation.

Pat employs all the exposition items we listed, however it is not always appropriate (or necessary) to do so. *Focusing on one strong item in the narrative can be as effective.* Pat's story is a good example of choosing the important and relevant things to include in a presentation. Sorting the important and relevant from the unimportant is a key skill of a designer. One way to decide what is important and relevant is to figure out the project's milestone moments. Milestones are specific moments in your process that relate specifically to a breakthrough in the design. You can weave milestone moments throughout your narrative.

Student Example

Let's look at an example of using breakthroughs in presentations in action using Alex, another fictitious student:

Alex's project is to create a brand for a mining company. During the design phase, Alex found a collection of old mining maps and surveys that contained beautiful drawings with intricate lines and contours. Alex used these maps as inspiration for the visual system. The design contained graphics developed from the contours and other visual elements in the maps. Finding the maps was a milestone moment that Alex chose to craft the presentation

A topology map like this one inspired the student in the example.

narrative around. Alex chose this milestone because it showed a direct cause and effect relationship in the design process, giving the audience an insight into the meaning and derivation of the design.

Along with the maps and surveys, Alex found countless other things that could have become inspiration for the design, however it is not advisable to include all of that in the presentation as well. The goal is not to show all the time and effort put into the design, but to choose the most relevant and connected example to build the narrative around.

Ideally your audience is more awake than this one.

No one likes to sit and listen to a 'laundry list' of excessive detail. People do not have long attention spans so you should form a concise and engaging narrative. Students often make the mistake of making long and overly complicated presentation narratives to try to prove how hard they worked. Fearing that if they do not describe the countless hours of work and every detail of their project their teacher will not appreciate how hard they worked. Instead you should assume that hard work and attention to detail is a baseline expectation for a designer, so you do not need to explain all this work. Unfortunately, a presentation filled with lots of the stories of struggles, problems and less relevant details of your design process will not only be too long, but it will not engage your audience either.

Online design students are not physically in the same room to stand up in front of the class. This makes the files and text submitted with an assignment especially important. Successful online students put time into crafting succinct descriptions of their work, and in making presentations like PDF files function without someone physically there to present. Labels, titles and explanatory notes can and should be used to help guide the viewer. Creating an easily navigable file will take extra time, so when you are online, build extra time into creating and presenting work. One advantage of online learning in terms of presentation is that it mirrors the profession. Designers very often send a PDF to a client in an email, so learning how to craft a good explanation that anticipates questions and persuades the viewer is a valuable skill.

Once you have presented (or submitted) your final project, deployment is over, but that is not necessarily the end of a project. In the professional world you may be debriefed about the success (or not) of a project, but in design school you get direct information about success (or not): an assessment and a grade. Good or bad, how do you make sense of your results and what can you learn from them? Because design is subjective you might also have questions about how your teacher comes up with the grade. So we will finish up this chapter talking about assessment, starting with the people who judge your work.

DESIGN JURIES, PANELS, COMMITTEES AND CLIENTS

While you are in design school you may have the opportunity to present your work in front of a jury. The word 'jury' sounds official, and possibly scary, and this is understandable. Most people who find themselves in front of a jury are in a legal situation, but in design school a jury is not punitive and there are no life sentences or fines to pay once a decision is made. A design jury is simply a group of experts who are gathered together to pass judgement on design work. Juries may be called 'panels' or 'committees'. Presenting to a jury has some similarities to presenting to clients.

What is a design jury and how are they usually put together?

Design juries are assembled for various reasons. For design competitions and shows, a jury will decide who participates and/or wins award(s). In graduate school a jury is usually referred to as a panel or a committee

Design jury meets and discusses student presentation.

who reviews and approves thesis projects. Although rare in graphic design studio classes, some graphic design teachers will assemble a small jury, often called a panel, to determine grades at the end of a class.

Most design juries are comprised of people you already know such as your teacher or other faculty members. Design school juries may also be comprised of outside experts, mostly designers, although sometimes a non-designer expert in a specific topic area will be included. Jury members are invited to evaluate work because they bring in an outsider's perspective, they are usually not familiar with your work before they see your presentation. This unfamiliarity is both a challenge and an opportunity. There are no preconceived notions, no understanding of the process that produced the work, so your work will succeed or not succeed entirely on its own merits, and on how well you present.

No matter who makes up your design jury panel, your goal is the same. You want 'buy-in' and 'sign-off'. A buy-in is the same as the professional world, it means the jury understands and likes what you have done. A 'sign-off' is when you receive a passing grade for the class, or approval for your project to pass. If the jury is judging a competition, then the buy-in and sign-off will mean recognition and an award.

The problem with design juries

Because they are made up of different types of people, and design is subjective, you may get conflicting feedback from a jury. This is something that tends to happen any time a group of people with different opinions, likes, dislikes and experiences are put together in one room. Designers are especially opinionated people. This is the strength of a jury too, having different passionate people in the room will allow for multiple ideas and perspectives, meaning juries are capable of giving you very good information about your work.

Most design juries deliberate in private, which allows for a free discussion. Jury discussion can be messy, it can be unclear what the outcome should be, and often it is the experience or perspectives of individual members that helps the jury to come to a consensus. Juries can be something like a shark tank, where the strongest member's view will win. If the jury deliberates in front of you then you will see and hear feedback on what they think you did well, what needs work, and what possibilities they see for your project.

Even though the people in a design jury have different opinions, dislikes and experiences, they also have a shared experience that comes from being in the world of design. Remembering this is useful: you share the common experience of being a designer. This means you can count on jury members agreeing on the basic design principles – that good design is based on exploration and research, understanding the audience and context. So, if you made appropriate design decisions and your work reflects a solid design process you can expect widespread agreement and a positive outcome.

Listening and responding to feedback from a jury

When you present to a jury there are usually two separate parts of the communication. The first is during the presentation when jury members ask you questions. The second is after a design jury has deliberated and you can ask questions.

Often students are very nervous about the outcome and as a result become distracted and less able to ask good questions or hear the underlying meaning of the answers. Students can often be emotional about the things they hear. You have a lot invested in your work, you care about it, and so it is natural to have anxiety and nervousness about people evaluating your work right in front of you. Remember design feedback is never personal. If you have this in mind when listening and responding to a jury, you will get a more out of the experience. Most students are anxious and may not remember what was said after the meeting is done. So, it is a very good idea to audio record or take notes (or have someone take notes for you) while the jury is providing feedback to you. Your goal is to get the information you need to succeed and to get sign-off. To do this you need to respond directly to the design issues the jury raises.

There are literally hundreds of possible ways that a jury member may form questions for you. Members of a design jury will often ask questions for clarification if they feel they do not have enough information, or are not clear about something you did or said. A jury member may not have heard a key piece of information and may ask you to simply restate or show something again. You may have shown or described something in a way that was not clear or additional information was needed. Asking questions is totally normal and does not necessarily mean your project or presentation is bad.

Many students sit passively as jury members throw tons of ideas at them in response to their work. Others can get upset and argue. It is okay to defend your work, but try to respond in a way that is respectful to the time and effort the jury has made to be there. Jury members do want you to succeed, so try not to respond with defensiveness and anger if you do not like what they are saying. Anger is counterproductive. You will most likely see these same jury members in class, or even professionally, at some point so, it is important to maintain a good working relationship.

How does a design jury compare to practice?

A professional presentation and a school design jury presentation are similar in that as a presenter you seek buy-in and sign-off from a group of people. The main differences between the two situations is the design knowledge of people in the room, and their relationship to you as the presenter.

In a professional presentation you are employed and are (usually) being paid for your work. Some of the people listening may be designers, but most of them are probably not – there may be brand managers, sales people, secretaries, CEOs, etc. As a designer you are employed to create communication that meets their needs, and they care only about the viability of the work you are producing, and its potential to advance their

As a professional designer you will often be tasked with presenting to non-designers.

marketing goals. Put simply: it is all business. They are not invested in your personal success in the same way a design school jury is.

Because many people on a professional design jury are not designers, you will need to craft a presentation that speaks to them in the right tone and with the right content. Do not assume the audience will understand the basic concepts of design thinking or that they have any visual understanding of what makes good or bad design. Be prepared for questions and feedback that is not focused on design ideas; you may be required to be somewhat of a teacher yourself.

This description may make a professional design jury presentation seem to be a harsh and cold environment compared to the warmer and friendlier design school jury. This may or may not be true. A professional audience will often have very nice people in it and can be quite friendly. Occasionally, a design school jury can be harsh and lack empathy. No two design jury experiences are the same. The best way to approach any design jury is to be positive, respectful and open to feedback. Juries can collectively contribute to a grade, so now let's talk about how grades can be determined.

UNDERSTANDING YOUR GRADE

Understanding the reasons for the grade helps you to improve your future work. In this section we unpack some of the factors around design studio grades. We cannot speak for every design teacher and school; all design teachers have grading criteria that are based on the project, and usually (or at least partly) set by the school. But there are common ways design teachers assess student work, and also common student concerns about evaluation. We explain and suggest solutions for both here, but this is general information. It is always a good idea to have a respectful conversation with your teacher about your grade. These conversations can help you learn as much about what you did right as what you did wrong.

Ultimately, the success of a project is directly related to process. It is rare that a student has great process and a poor outcome. Doing great work in your research, sketching, exploration, development and production (almost always) assures you will get a good final assessment and grade. Conversely, poor process pretty much always results in poor assessments.

Just as when making good sushi, making good design requires excellent ingredients, skill, and attention to detail.

So, the first thing to understand about your grade is that if you have been appropriately working through your ideas, you should be heading for a passing result. Conversely, if you skipped steps, or did not apply yourself fully to the process, you should expect poor assessment results. If the result is poor and you know that you did not fully apply yourself to the process there is nothing you can do after the fact, but you can change the way you approach your design process going forward.

There can be differences between how a student feels they progressed through a project and what the teacher has observed. Asking your teacher for their assessment of your process during the project rather than at the end can help you determine where you may be strong or weak, so you can adjust before the final is due.

All design teachers place value on the design process, but be clear about how much your teacher values process versus outcomes. Do they give a grade for process? How much (the weight) of the overall grade is process? If this is not made clear in the class outline or brief you should ask.

Effort versus results

Effort doesn't equal success. Say you worked hard on your project, put in late nights, and made many revisions, but your assessment and final grade is not great. How can this happen? Doesn't more time and effort always equal better work? Sadly not. Often effort goes together with success but not always. Problems arise when students confuse mere time spent working on a project with time spent in the right way on the right things.

Student Example

Let's return to fictitious student Pat to explain some of this dynamic of spending time the right way.

Pat is a diligent, hard worker, who works on projects late into the night, helps out classmates and is highly active in critique. Pat thinks about homework during the day, even when doing things that are not design related. Despite all of this time and effort, Pat's work is still not great, and neither are Pat's grades.

In one particular class Pat was struggling to create a visual system for a presentation video. Pat's visual quality was weak both aesthetically and conceptually. The instructor gave Pat comprehensive feedback and suggested some ideas that could be explored to raise the quality of the visuals. Pat found this advice difficult and circled around and around before deciding to work on the text for the script instead. The writing took a lot of time as Pat was not the best writer, but at the end of the week the script was okay. However, Pat submitted visual work in the next class session that was basically unchanged. Pat initially protested about 'working really hard late at night', but under questioning confessed to spending the majority of the week's time writing a script for the presentation.

Pat's issue is a common one. By working hard on the writing and not exploring the concepts and visuals, Pat had worked hard, he had effectively stalled the project. Where you place your effort matters just as much as how much effort you put in. Focusing on less difficult or less important parts of the work delays working on the important parts of the project. Spending a lot of time on less important tasks can feel like a lot of effort, so this dynamic is deceptive and easy to slip into. Time spent on the wrong things is a self-defeating strategy leading to incomplete or unrefined final projects and consequently poor grades. Be honest with yourself when you are working. If you fall into this trap next time try 'working smart'. Figure out the strategically most important aspects of the project and focus there. Give minimal time to the less important things. If you do not know what more or less important parts of the project are, then ask your teacher.

Being active in class critique and offering help to your fellow students like Pat does is valuable. You will learn how to evaluate and to speak about design. However, some students are better at talking about design than designing and find themselves with disappointing grades. Offering advice is great, but remember to apply that advice to your own work and be aware that this can be surprisingly hard to do. It is often easier to tell other people what to do with their work than apply a critical lens to our own work. Improving depends upon learning to self-critique, so work actively on this skill.

To get better grades your work has to materially improve. 'Spinning your wheels' is the term we use when you are putting out a lot of effort but not going anywhere, just like a car stuck in the mud. Working without your work getting better can be extremely frustrating. However, rather than not addressing the key issues in your work, try some of the techniques we talked about in Chapter 3 to deal with stuckness. It's better to try different approaches to the important parts of the process than to work on something else.

Subjectivity in assessment

The design studio classroom is just like any other place in the social world; people have likes, and dislikes and emotions. In many other pursuits these things don't impact your grade but not so in graphic design. No matter how much information is on a rubric or described in the brief, ultimately your work will be assessed (at least in part) by your teacher's taste. For example, if a teacher thinks that landscape-oriented (horizontal) books are less professional than portrait oriented (vertical) books, and you decide to go with a landscape format, you will struggle to get a good grade regardless of how well you executed the design. Pay attention to what your teacher shows you, especially graded examples (exemplar) of work so you understand what they are looking for.

Both of these images are of classic German cars that represent two very different design tastes.

On the face of it, basing grades subjectively rather than by objective criteria sounds terrible, but recall that we have talked about taste and the design eye in previous chapters. Design is inevitably subjective, but your teacher's design eye is connected to the professional world, their taste comes from practice. In fact, a large benefit of going to design school is being exposed to the taste of other designers.

You will not always agree with your teacher's taste, indeed some of the most famous designers disagreed with their teachers and proved them wrong, but they are the exception that proves the rule. You should respect and understand your teacher's subjectivity just as you have to respect a creative director when you start working as a designer. Design teachers are placed in the role for their knowledge, opinions and their taste in design, so trusting this is key. Having said that, this does not mean you should never question your grade. At the very least, questioning a grade will allow you further understanding of how that grade was derived. No grade is entirely arbitrary or based solely on the teacher's likes and dislikes – it will have a connection to the project goal. Your teacher should be able to clearly articulate how your work does and does not measure up.

WHAT IS YOUR TEACHER LOOKING FOR?

In the following pages are a variety of examples to help you see different types of presentations in different contexts.

- Professional style presentation
- Using a narrative
- A slide presentation
- Online presentation

Case study

PROFESSIONAL STYLE PRESENTATION

A professional style presentation is about efficiency and focus. The best professional presentations move quickly through the background and reasoning and into the tangible results of the project.

Title: Brand Rescue Project

Level & subject: Advanced, Branding Design

University: Ferris State University, USA

Teachers: Alison Pop and Nic Mata

Deliverable: The final is a professional presentation using a slide deck. In the presentation are the design brief and brand strategy document, which includes a user scenario, user archetypes and diagram with experience model. Process work showing the development of the brand concept, logo and visual system and the branded environment are also included.

PROJECT DESCRIPTION

In this senior level project, students team up to develop a branded experience for a restaurant. The goal of the project is to design from an experiential perspective, using strategic thinking, creative concepts and displaying technical skills. Students begin the

discover phase by researching retail, dining and mobile media interaction and writing a brief. In design and development students are urged to consider the senses (sight, sound, touch, taste and smell) and the user's inner feelings.

──── HOW TO SUCCEED IN A PROFESSIONAL STYLE PRESENTATION

The instructions for the project in this case study illustrate how close a professional presentation can be to a design school presentation:

- Organize, format and present all components of your solution.

- Have your printed manual for examination at your presentation.

- Entertain and inform.

- Have your confidence on display.

These are all things a professional designer would do before (and during) a presentation.

The directions for the presentation are concise, however what the instructors are looking for is more involved than it may appear. Alison and Nic direct their students to understand the audience for the presentation, and deliver information that meets their needs, and to be clear in presenting their work and the value it provides to the client. Meaning that they want students to consider what to include and what to leave out from the perspective of the audience, not themselves. Alison and Nic illustrate this point by saying, 'Your audience may not know or care what a mood board provides, depending on their background and/or goals because anything not specifically for the client has no business in a professional presentation.' Only present content that has a direct link to the requirements and goals of the project as stated in the brief.

Alison and Nic give the following helpful advice for a professional style presentation:

Practice! Time is valuable to everyone, so get used to keeping the clock running in the back of your mind.

Learn to distinguish. Sometimes it's helpful to refocus and get things back on track.

Be flexible. In some environments your presentation is one-sided, while in others it is conversational. Be able to adapt to questions and turns in conversation quickly.

Be confident. You're making recommendations based on your process and problem-solving ability. If you have done the work be proud of it.

Opposite: Student work by Mckenna Mcintyre, Connor Vondette and Allie Crippen.

Student work by Mckenna Mcintyre, Connor Vondette and Allie Crippen.

Alison and Nic advise students to show and not tell, meaning as visual people, designers should strive to represent ideas through images, not through lengthy descriptions. Indeed many students make the mistake of talking a lot during a presentation, believing it will demonstrate knowledge, or mask a lack of ideas, or design (or a lack of confidence in them). As Alison and Nic point out, designers are training to be clear on the entire process and be able to speak to the overall solution. So get to the point in an engaging way as seamlessly (and quickly) as possible.

WHAT YOUR TEACHER IS EXPECTING

Teachers look for a presentation that is focused and directed to the design outcomes from the perspective of the client. To do this, present a minimal amount of process and exploration, use only the material that directly connects to the project goals.

Case study

USING A NARRATIVE

A narrative presentation uses a story to engage the audience. A persona can be utilized in a narrative to help the audience understand the design solution from the user's perspective.

Title: Inclusive Museum Project for the North Carolina Museum of Natural Sciences (NCMNS)

Level & subject: Advanced, Experience Design

University: North Carolina State University, USA

Teachers: Helen Armstrong

Deliverable: Research and design for the assistive tool and a final presentation to the stakeholders from the NCMNS. Each keynote presentation had to be completed with a 10–15 minute time limit and covered an introduction to the persona, a user journey map, and included a short scenario video. In addition, each student team prepared a poster detailing the project to leave behind with the client.

PROJECT DESCRIPTION

Students were teamed up in groups to work with the client, North Carolina Museum of Natural Sciences (NCMNS), to create inclusive experience design solutions for the museum's 'The Terror of the South' dinosaur exhibition. Because the project is for a real-world client, the blended brief was open in terms of the final product but tightly defined in terms of the problem, client and audience. The goal was to develop an assistive tool to transform the exhibition into an autism-friendly experience. This proposed tool (either phone, tablet-based, physical artefact or other embedded technology) was customized to better serve the needs of young adult visitors on the autism spectrum.

HOW TO SUCCEED IN A NARRATIVE PRESENTATION

This case study is a good example of how to structure a narrative presentation that is clear, comprehensible and engaging. Helen's instructions to the students is a sequence that can be adapted to many kinds of projects:

Hook (optional): Begin with a short anecdote about one of your specific experiences working on the project. In other words, begin with a little story.

Persona details…: 'Let me introduce you to…', who are they, what are their needs, how will they be visiting the museum?

User journey: Take us through their visit to the museum, pointing out along the way how your concept is meeting their needs.

Short scenario video: Take us through your concept from the perspective of the persona.

Sum up your concept in one slide: What is the most important way that your concept meets your user's needs?

Scalability: How can your concept be used by other museums or other public spaces?

For reflection: End your presentation with one to two ideas for further reflection. In other words, if you could spend more time working on this project, what would you like to think more about?

Helen specifically encourages students to describe the persona(s), so the audience can clearly form a mental picture and the students can then lead the audience through a journey, saying: 'The student's job is to help us get inside the head of their persona and empathize with his/her needs. We need to see their project in action during the presentation in order to understand it'. Although personas and user journeys are typically used in UX projects, these methods can be useful for a wide range of design projects.

Multiple pieces of design can be presented seamlessly and cohesively by leading audiences through a journey (and story). The narrative sequence can be a story with several smaller distinct stories inside. Each smaller story plays a role in providing the background, information and design solution while engaging (and hopefully entertaining) the audience. Multiple deliverables and ideas can be presented as storylines. In this presentation the storylines culminate in a short scenario video, which allows the audience to see the project design unfold from the point of view of the persona as they interact with the design.

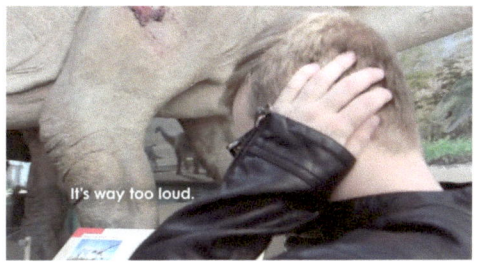

Video stills from student presentation.

Helen provides good advice to make a story come alive when you are in front of the audience: 'Presentations should be well rehearsed and succinct but never read. They should be performed.' Helen has her students practise by giving their presentations ahead of time in class to gather feedback, and then refine before presenting to the client.

WHAT YOUR TEACHER IS EXPECTING

Treat your teacher like a client and audience member. Think about what they want to hear and what they might best respond to and weave the story around that. No audience, including your teacher, wants to watch a boring presentation – aim to perform the presentation, don't just read it.

Case study

A SLIDE PRESENTATION

In a slide presentation content, design, presenter delivery, and presenter appearance all work in harmony to tell a coherent, engaging story that elicits a positive emotional response in viewers.

Title: Data Visualization for Social Engagement

Level & subject: Beginning, Information Design

University: University of Nevada, USA

Teacher: Dr Katherine Hepworth

Deliverable: The visualization may be in chart, symbol, or text form, or a combination of all three. The promotional item may incorporate other elements such as coding, photography and video as supplemental elements. The final is a persuasive slide presentation given to the class.

PROJECT DESCRIPTION

The goal of this project is to use the foundational principles of ethical data visualization to analyse and share knowledge with an audience. Students are teamed up to develop persuasive, data-driven, promotional items by analysing data sources from a not-for-profit organization. Each team researches, designs and produces at least one promotional item that relies on data visualization for its effectiveness.

HOW TO SUCCEED WITH A SLIDE PRESENTATION

Katherine relates the creation of a slide presentation to the way a playwright crafts a play, because the information on the slides has to combine with the speaker's performance. She says, 'When a playwright writes a play, they need to keep many elements in mind in order to prepare a really evocative script: the actors' speaking voices and movements, costumes, the stage, and the set. Envision what physical movement will accompany your slides, along with what you say, and how you will say it. Gestures, speed and tone of voice convey a lot of extra communication. Imagine your body (movement), voice (the script), stage (the room), set (the slides), and costume (personal appearance) as elements in one integrated performance.'

A slide presentation is a performance, and Katherine suggests that to be successful students should adopt the mindset of a performer or actor. Performing can produce anxiety, but as Katherine observes, it is normal for even the most seasoned actors to feel nerves before and during a performance, and so you will likely feel nervous before and during your presentation delivery. The trick of great actors is to use that nervous energy as fuel for giving a great performance.

Katherine says that presentation takes preparation to do well. Many elements – speech, physical movement, slide content, slide design and presentation technology – need to be coordinated to run smoothly on the day. The best way to ensure a trouble-free delivery is to make a draft of your slides well before the final presentation day, and then rehearse your delivery many times. The first rehearsals can be done on your own without presentation technology (such as a projector), and will help you see where you have major errors in terms of structure and timing. After you have sorted through these major errors, try to rehearse in a room with a projector, to an audience of at least one friend.

Bringing in an audience is very helpful, Katherine says, and she suggests that you should ask your audience to let you know what doesn't make sense to them. Don't just ask your audience for feedback – Katherine recommends you observe their reaction: 'Your audience will also look more and less engaged at various points in your rehearsal. Both your rehearsal audience's comments and reactions provide valuable information about what to change in a future rehearsal. Your rehearsing is complete when your rehearsal audience is engaged all the way through, and you are confident in your material and timing.'

WHAT YOUR TEACHER IS EXPECTING

Teachers understand that you may be nervous, they do not judge you for this, so try not to let your nerves get the better of you. But no one, including teachers, likes to watch a presenter get lost and flail around, so make it a strong performance and practise, practise, practise!

Case study

ONLINE PRESENTATION

Online presentations need to be carefully constructed to speak for your work and answer questions even though you may not be there. As a consequence, preparing an online presentation can take extra time.

Title: Conference Event Design

Level & subject: Intermediate, Event Design

University: Academy of Art University, USA

Teacher: William Culpepper

Deliverable: A brand and brand architecture applied to the following set of event materials: website, brochure, way finding, give-aways and event uniforms. For the final presentation video students use screen capture software to capture voice-over while clicking through a PDF of their work. The student submits the file for teacher review through a learning management system. This means students do not present to their teacher in person.

PROJECT DESCRIPTION

This blended brief directs students to create a set of materials for a conference. The goal of the project is to create a brand and visual system that works across an integrated set of print and digital deliverables. The final deliverables are presented as a short video with a voice-over narrative.

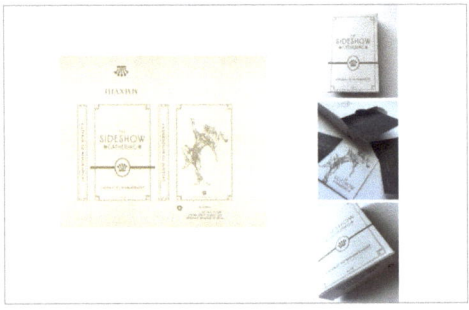

Images of slideshow from a student final presentation.

HOW TO SUCCEED AT AN ONLINE PRESENTATION

Most online presentations are done asynchronously, so student and teacher are not together in space and time, but the basic tenants of presenting that you have seen in the previous case studies still apply, as this case study shows. 'In an online presentation there is usually less pressure and nerves than an in-person presentation,' says William. Those students who feel uncomfortable speaking in front of others, usually feel more comfortable speaking in front of a computer, and in their own space. Regardless, William advises students to pretend as if this final presentation was to an actual client and says that a trial run always helps put the student more at ease – sometimes several trial runs are needed.

William suggests that writing a script that correlates with the visual presentation is very helpful and allows students to create a more focused presentation. Students can also try using on-screen notes instead of memorizing, which is helpful for students who have limited presentation experience. Notes allow the presentation and topic to stay on track, focused and concise. However, William reminds students not to read from notes: otherwise this creates a monotone voice that will put everyone watching asleep. Creating a performance is still as important even when you are not presenting live in person.

William gives his recorded online students the same advice as he does for an in-person presentation: 'It's important to speak clearly, enunciate, and remember to speak slowly.' William recommends online students buy a microphone or headset, instead of using a built-in computer microphone. 'Microphones are the most important element in an online presentation,' says William, 'because they allow the presenter's voice to be clear and easy to hear'.

When it comes to content, William suggests that students keep the presentation direct, to the point and short. Instead of stating what is already shown, William suggests that students focus on the concepts and why the design choices were made.

WHAT YOUR TEACHER IS EXPECTING

You may have more time to prepare and practice with an online presentation, so the expectations can be higher. Don't leave putting your presentation together until the last minute, even if it is a simple presentation PDF. Remember to use labels and titles to guide the viewer, as you may not be there live to explain everything.

See and read the entire brief and see student examples at:
www.bloomsbury.com/the-graphic-design-process-9781350050785

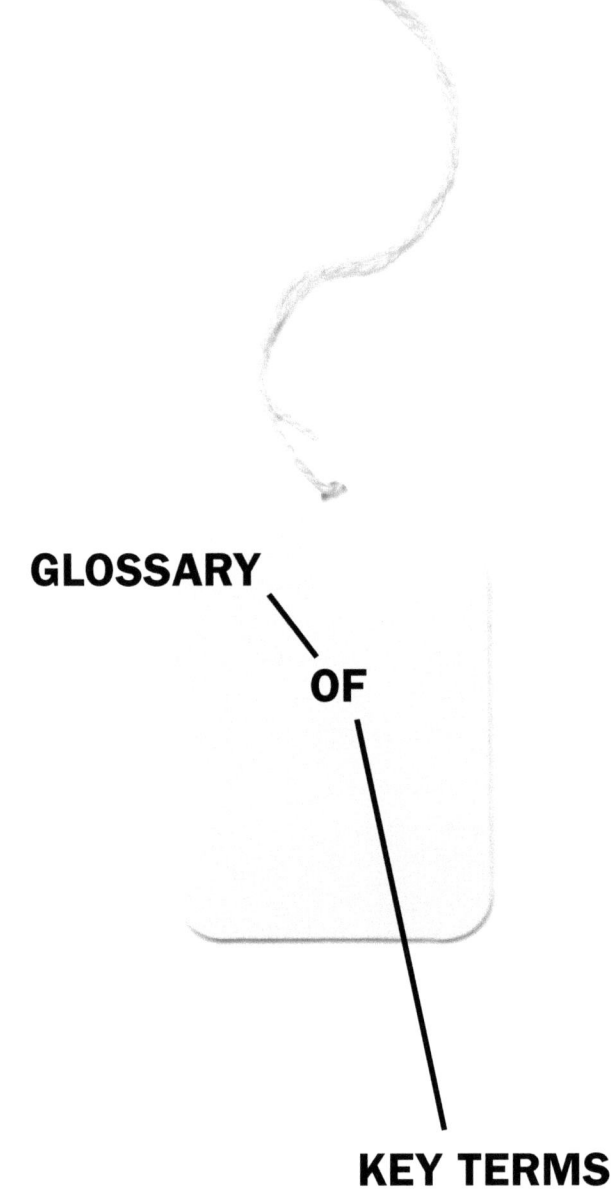

GLOSSARY OF KEY TERMS

Graphic design uses some words and terms in ways different to the dictionary definition. We used plain language throughout the book, but we could not avoid using some of these terms. As these may be unfamiliar to the beginning designer this glossary will help you better understand the book (and your design teacher). Here, we explain all of the terms we did not define in the text.

Aesthetics: What a design looks like in terms of style and/or quality. If your teacher says 'there's a problem with your aesthetics' means your design is not good quality. If they say: "you could use an Art Deco aesthetic here" it means use a style: i.e. make the design, look like Art Deco.

Brand: Commonly used to refer to the logo that represents a product, service or company. To designers the term encompasses the image, message, positioning and audience's emotional responses as well as the associated visual system that accompanies most logos.

Cliché (Visual Cliché): A visual that is a tired, worn out, expected and obvious way to represent something (i.e. using a picture of a lightbulb to represent 'an idea'). A cliché is the opposite of what designers call a 'fresh' idea, which is any design/visual that is new or unique.

Comp(s): Short for 'comprehensive' which in pre-computer times was artwork assembled to show the client what a final design would look like. Technically, a comp is the final design artwork for your project. However, a comp can refer to the design variations produced during development, which show what the design could look like. The words 'drafts', 'comps', 'mock-ups', 'layout', 'prototypes', 'rough' and 'dummy are used somewhat interchangeably. Most comps will be a printout or PDF, but the term is also used for 3D items such as a package or a book.

Component(s): When a design has several parts, each individual part will be referred to as a component. For example, an ad campaign that has several different ad formats like a billboard, online and print ad has 'multiple components'.

Concept (also: Idea, Design Concept, Design Idea): A concept is an idea and plan for a design. Concept can also be used as another term for aesthetics, or visuals, usually called a 'formal concept'. For example, a formal concept to make a cookbook like a technical manual is an idea for making a set of visuals that look a certain way. A concept is the idea a viewer forms in their mind when they see a visual. Many advertisements and logos work this way, using a visual to stand in for something else so that the viewer can make a connection and then understand the idea. This kind of concept is often called a 'conceptual idea'. The term 'Conceptual' is often used to describe an idea or design that is very abstract or obscure – being told your design is 'too' or 'very' conceptual is not always a compliment, as it usually means the design is not easily understandable.

Craft: Craft is the finish on a design, which comes from how well constructed it is. If you are making a package craft will refer to how well the material is cut, folded and glued together. In a digital file, craft will refer to how precisely the artwork is positioned. Also, a term for design skill, i.e. 'Sanjay really knows his craft'.

Creative Director (CD): In the hierarchy of a design studio the CD is the leader of the designers. Sometimes called an Art Director or Design Director, the CD makes the creative decisions. A Senior Designer (sometimes called an Art Director) is a more experienced designer.

Criteria: The standard(s) by which a design is judged.

Decorate/Decoration/Decorative: Anything added to a design to 'make it more interesting' but does not support the concept or enhance the aesthetics. Elements may be decorative (embellished, or obviously pretty), but not decoration as long as they support the concept or enhance the design. Elements (Photoshop filters for example) added just because you like them, or because they are currently trendy, or you think they are cool, are decoration. Being told your design is decorative is usually code for 'clean it up and make it simpler'.

Design Direction: The concept and aesthetics of a piece of design. During convergent thinking a final design direction is chosen and the designer will make a series of variations of that direction to produce the final artwork.

Development (Interactive): The process of coding and testing used to create an interactive product such as a website or app.

Digital Tools (Tools): Computer applications used to produce graphic design, for example Adobe Creative Suite. Digital Prototyping (for example Sketch) tools allow designers to show how interactive projects work without coding.

Drafts (also Computer Drafts): A version of the design produced during the design and develop part of the process which will be critiqued and adjusted. Drafts can be done as pencil sketches or on the computer (See Comps).

Element(s) (also Graphic Forms): Any distinct piece or component that makes up a piece of graphic design. Images, logos, headlines, shapes and patterns etc. are all elements. The term graphic form is sometimes used to mean an element, but a graphic form may refer to a group of elements, or even to the whole design.

Exercise: As distinct from an assignment or project, an activity to help build design and/or tool skills. Because an exercise is for skill building, not for show, it will not usually be finished to a high standard.

Final Art: The artwork sent to a printer. In design school this is the very final of a design project, which is technically a comp as final art for printing may not look like the final. Final Art must be perfect.

Finish (also Fit and Finish): Completeness, quality and precision of a design. Design that is not quite ready for production yet or is badly produced does not have sufficient fit and finish. Non-professional design, which looks amateur, does not have a high standard of finish. Finish also refers to effects applied to printed materials, such as embossing or foil stamping.

First-Year: Beginning designer, equivalent of a Freshman in the US college system. A second-year is a Sophomore, third-year a Junior (or Senior depending on the length of the program), and a Final-year is a Senior.

Focal Point: Place (or places) that are the most important and first to draw the viewer's eye in a design.

Formal/Formal Skills: Formal is another word for visual, as in a 'formal idea' (see concept). Formal skills are the generally accepted practical skills designers possess to successfully manipulate the elements and principles of design to create a design.

Format: The nature (printed or interactive), materials (i.e. paper, plastic etc.), shape, size and finish of the design.

Frame (Key Frame): A motion design term for a static piece of art that defines the start/finish of a motion design sequence.

Functionality (also Interaction/ Interactivity): The actions, affordances and capabilities of a design or format. Functionality may describe how an interactive design works, or how a package opens as well as the intended purpose or goal of a piece of graphic design.

Go Live: The deadline for when an interactive product such as an app or website is released.

Hierarchy: The order of importance of elements in a design. Effective hierarchy means the viewer looks at the elements in the desired sequence, from most to least important.

High/Low-End Design: Expensive looking/ less expensive (not expensive or even cheap) looking.

Imagery: Any visual such as photographs, illustrations, or patterns used in a design.

Insight(s): A discovery, or deep and/or new understanding about a subject that can spark ideas for, or a way to approach, a design project.

Journey Map: a UX term for diagramming how a person works through/with a digital product such as an app or website.

Line Spacing (also Leading): The space between lines of type.

Marketing/Marketer: Marketing is the content/practice to sell/promote a company, product or service. Marketing has 'messaging' which is the information the client wants the audience to know

Materials (also Media): The stuff a design is composed of – for example the materials used to compose this book are paper (and ink). Media is what the design is transported or carried through, for example the media for a website is the Internet, the media for a book is print.

Motion Design: Using the graphic design elements and principles for film and video production. Motion design often animates type.

Online/Blended (also Hybrid) Learning: Online learning is mediated through a web-based portal called a Learning Management System (LMS). Fully online learning is generally asynchronous – student and teacher do not meet in real time. Blended learning combines online with in-person/in-time meetings in a classroom or through a video conferencing system.

Outcomes (also Deliverables): The products of a graphic design assignment or brief.

Overwork: Messing around with a design so long that you lose your way and cannot see/find what is good about the design anymore.

Pacing (also Progression or Moves): The flow and timing of a design (or presentation). Good pacing has rhythm and repetition to seem consistent but with enough variation to make the piece interesting. Pacing can be simple or complex, boring or interesting.

Palette: A selected group of colors that are used consistently throughout a design because they work harmoniously (or communicate a brand).

Parameters: The restrictions and challenges of a project, some visual and some functional, related to materials, size, format etc. Parameters must be worked with, and pushed to the limits, but never ignored.

Pedagogy: The function and methods of teaching. Design studio pedagogy is an 'active pedagogy' where students work on projects with input from teachers, rather than listen to lectures and then write essays.

Point Size: Measure of type size: roughly 1/72nd of an inch or 0.353 millimeters.

Polish/Polished: A description of the professionalism, quality and completeness of a design. Design that is pleasing and executed with accuracy and precision has a high level of polish. Work that is sloppy and has typos has a low level of polish. The words polish and high-end are sometimes used interchangeably.

Portfolio (also Folio or Book): A collection of a designer's work, which is carefully curated and arranged to best represent a designer's skill. Portfolios are the only way designers can show what they can do to potential employers. Always back up your work in design school – it is literally your tuition made visible.

Positioning: A marketing term indicating the way a product, service or company etc. compares to its competitors in the mind of the audience.

Practice: Professionally working/the workplace of a graphic designer.

Product (also Digital Product): As distinct from a traditional product that needs packaging a product or digital product is the term used for a digital platform, website, application or experience. An app is a product, a social media platform is a product. Graphic designers who specialize in this kind of design call themselves product designers.

Production: The process and work of making a design real. For printing this means creating print-ready artwork. For a digital product production will include making visuals along with the development work. In design school production means making the final comp.

Prototypes: Full-scale, working model of a design, a series of prototypes can be used to test and refine a design (see Comp).

Roughs (also Rough Ideas, Initial Ideas): The very first sketches or computer drafts of a design. Roughs are quickly made and discarded in the early stages of the design phase.

Scale: Relative proportion of design elements. Scale can be used to create focal points and hierarchy.

Slide(s): A single page of a presentation created in an application like Keynote and PowerPoint.

Social, Social Context: Design that relates to people and communities. Designing for social good means designing to benefit a group of people, designing for a social issue means designing to solve for a problem experienced by a group of people.

Solution (also Design Solution): A finished design, the answer to a design problem as posed by a brief.

Stakeholders: The people involved or concerned with a design or situation but not the direct audience for, or directly affected by, a design.

Strategy: A plan of attack (tactics are the things done to execute a plan of attack). In graphic design a strategy is the whole proposed solution to the design problem.

Technical: The practical skill and details that go into creating a finished design. Usually refers to using a computer but not always. Having technical skill means you can use tools (digital or analogue) quickly and accurately to create precise artwork or mockups.

Technique: A skill-based way of making something. Sometimes used interchangeably with craft. If a designer has 'good technique' it means that they can execute a design idea very well. Technique is important – a good design idea can be ruined if it is badly executed.

Typo: A mistake, which could be a misspelled word or incorrect sequence of letters or words.

Typography (also Type, Typographic): The practice of arranging and designing lettering. Typography is the defining characteristic/skill of graphic designers because we (almost) always have to design type, no matter what the project.

Usability: How easy it is to learn and use an interactive product.

User Experience (UX): UX is short for User Experience. User Experience is the practice of designing for interaction. Graphic designers who specialize in this area call themselves UX designers.

Users/User-Testing: The people who use and/or interact with a design. User-testing is the practice of improving a design by observing users interacting with the design.

Variations (also Variables): Slightly different designs based on the same design direction, which help to test and adjust different aspects of the design to get to the final version.

Visual Design: A UX term for creating and applying the visuals to an interactive design. Visual Designers work with UX designers to 'clothe' the product. Sometimes used to refer to the look and feel of a design as distinct from the concept or function of the design.

Visual System: A collection of elements (which may include images, elements, patterns etc.) that are used to make a design look consistent across one or more formats. A visual system includes the designer defined 'rules' of how the elements are to be arranged and combined.

Wireframe: A mock-up of a digital product that displays what will be on each screen

Workshopping: Working a design out by making and talking about the ideas/design with other people.

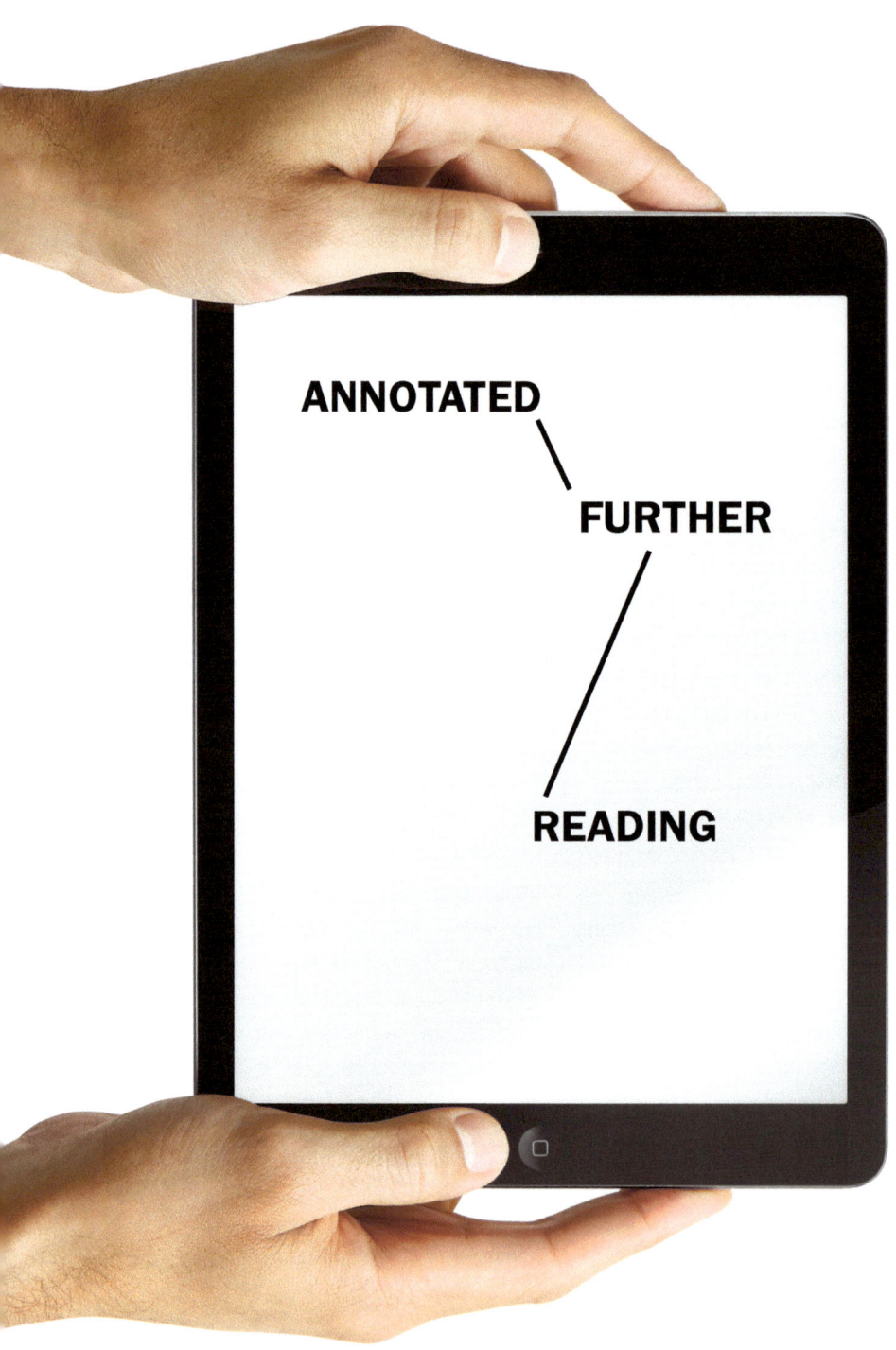

This list contains the most useful books on a range of topics relevant to this book.

The 'Graphic Design' books are a 'best of' list about the elements and principles of design, layout, typography, presentation, ideas and theory.

The 'Design Thinking' books explain the way designers think and work (and the way designers are taught).

We have included some of the best books we know about working as a designer in 'Design Careers' because it is never too early to start thinking about what comes after design school.

As promised, we include books about 'Semiotics'. This is a complicated subject, and these titles are the most easily understandable references.

Finally, there are many books about 'Creativity and Process'. We think the ones listed here are worth your time.

Graphic designers are somewhat famous for liking and collecting books – we hope some of these will make good additions to your library, whether it is small or extensive. Happy reading.

Graphic Design

Basics Graphic Design Box Set by Gavin Ambrose, Nigel Aono-Billson and Neil Leonard Fairchild Books, London, 2014

Universal Principles of Design (2nd Edition) by William Lidwell, Kristina Holden and Jill Butler Rockport Publishers, Beverly, MA, 2010

Thinking with Type: A Critical Guide for Designers, Writers, Editors & Students (2nd Edition) by Ellen Lupton Princeton Architectural Press, Hudson, New York, 2010

The Elements of Typographic Style (Fourth Edition) by Robert Bringhurst Hartley and Marks Publishers, Point Roberts, WA, 2013

Graphic Design Theory: Readings from the Field by Helen Armstrong Princeton Architectural Press, Hudson, New York, 2010

Designing the Editorial Experience: A primer for Print, Web and Mobile
By Sue Apfelbaum and Juliette Cezzar Rockport Publishers, Beverly, MA, 2014

Slide:ology: The Art and Science of Creating Great Presentations by Nancy Duarte O'Reilly Media, North Sebastopol, CA, 2008

Made to Stick: Why some ideas take hold and others become unstuck by Chip and Dan Heath Random House Books, London, 2007

How to be a Graphic Designer Without Losing Your Soul by Adrian Shaughnessy Princeton Architectural Press, Hudson, New York, 2010

The AIGA Guide to Careers in Graphic and Communication Design by Juliette Cezzar Bloomsbury Academic, London, 2017

Talent is not Enough: Business Secrets for Designers by Shel Perkins New Riders Publishing / Peachpit Press, San Francisco, 2005

Graphic Artist's Guild Handbook of Pricing and Ethical Guidelines (15th Edition) Graphic Artists Guild, New York, NY, 2018

Flaunt: Designing effective, compelling and memorable portfolios of creative work by Bryony Gomez-Palacio and Armin Vit UnderConsideration LLC, Austin, TX, 2010

Design Thinking

Change by Design: How Design Thinking Transforms by Tim Brown HarperCollins, New York, NY, 2009

The Design of Everyday Things by Don Norman Basic Books / Perseus Books Group, New York, NY, 2013

Design thinking for Visual Communication by Gavin Ambrose Bloomsbury Visual Arts, London, 2017

Educating the Reflective Practitioner: How Professionals Think in Action by Donald A Schön Jossey-Bass, San Francisco, CA, 1987

Design Thinking: Understanding How Designers Think and Work by Nigel Cross Bloomsbury Academic, London, UK, 2015

Sciences of the Artificial by Herbert A. Simon M.I.T, Boston, MA 1996

How Designers Think (4th Edition) by Bryan Lawson Routledge, New York, NY, 2005

Creativity and Process

Creative Connection Cards: A Toolkit for Creative Thinking By Anitra Nottingham and Jeremy Stout, creativeconnection.cards

The Design Process by Karl Aspelund Fairchild Books, London, 2015

The Mind Map Book: Unlock Your Creativity, Boost Your Memory, Change Your Life By Tony Buzan and Barry Buzan Pearson Education, Harlow, U.K., 2010

The Artists Way: A Spiritual Path to Higher Creativity by Julia Cameron Souvenir Press, London, U.K., 2012

Graphic Design Process: From Problem to Solution by Nancy Skolos and Thomas Wedell Laurence King Publishing London, U.K., 2012

Semiotics

Left to Right by David Crow AVA Publishing, Lausanne, Switzerland, 2006

Visible Signs by David Crow AVA Publishing, Lausanne, Switzerland, 2011

This Means This This Means That: A Users Guide to Semiotics by Sean Hall Laurence King Publishing, London, U.K., 2012

Understanding Comics: The Invisible Art by Scott McCloud William Morrow Paperbacks / HarperCollins, New York, NY, 1994

Note: Page numbers in italic refer to captions.

A

aesthetic descriptors 125
Armstrong, Helen 175–8
asking questions 127, 129
case study 133–5
audience perspective 50–1

B

benchmarking 13
Benson, Eric 61–3
books, recommended 190–3
brainstorming see divergent thinking
briefings 33
    visual examples 33–5
Buck-Coleman, Audra 64–7

C

Cezzar, Juliette 108–11
Chen, Yinzhi 56
committees see design juries
computer and pen sketching 95–7
content, creating 42–4
context, design problem 46–9
convergent thinking 25–6, 112–21
    being comfortable with uncertainty 119–20
    developing a 'design eye' 120–1
    keep going or start again 116–17
    problem spaces and problem space solutions 117–19
    student example 113–15
creative, learning to be 17–18
Crisp, Denise Gonzales 133–5
critique 11–13
    case study 139–42
    characteristics of good 127–9
    group/peer 12, 13, 122, 129–30
    group/peer case study 143–5
    methods 122–4
    'one-on-one' 12, 123
    online 12, 13, 123–4
    participation 130
    reframing 130–1
    student example 128
    subjectivity in 125–7
    working with 127–31
Culpepper, William 181–3

D

deep freeze 76
deployment phase 26, 146–69
    design juries 160–5
    presenting your work 148–60
    understanding your grade 165–9
deployment phase case studies 170–83
    online case study 181–3
    professional style presentation 171–4
    slide presentation case study 179–80
    using a narrative 175–8
design briefs 24, 32–3, 36–46
    blended case study 61–3
    creating content 42–4
    defining design problem 38–9
    defining success using 52–3
    design schools and different 45–6
    explorative case study 58–60
    items in professional 36–7
    loose case study 64–7
    loose versus tight 39–41, 52–3
    in practice versus design school 42–4
    tight case study 54–7
design constraints 38–9
'design eye,' developing a 120–1
design juries 160–5
    feedback 163–4
    presentations to professional and student 164–5
    problem with 162
    putting together of 160–2
design phase 24–5, 68–97
    divergent thinking 24–5, 69–77
    generating ideas 78–92
    sketches and drafts 92–7
design phase case studies 98–111
    divergent thinking 99–102
    loose sketches 103–7
    tight sketches 108–11
design problems
    from audience perspective 50–1
    context 46–9
    design brief defining 38–9
    presentation 153
    understanding 46–53
    'wicked' 117
design schools 7, 8–9, 10–13
    'portfolio' and 'process' 45–6

design thinking 15–16
    in graphic design 19–20
    learning to be creative 17–18
    messiness 20–2
designer talk, understanding 124–5
desk crit 123
details, paying attention to 150–2
development phase 25–6, 112–31
    convergent thinking 112–21
    working with critique 127–31
    working with your instructor 122–7
development phase case studies 132–45
    asking questions 133–5
    critique 139–42
    group critique 143–5
    subjectivity 136–8
discovery phase 23–4, 31–53
    design briefs 32–3, 36–46, 52–3
    design problem 46–53
    starting a project 32–5
discovery phase case studies 54–67
    blended brief 61–3
    explorative brief 58–60
    loose brief 64–7
    tight brief 54–7
divergent thinking 24–5, 69–77
    case study 99–102
    getting stuck 73–5
    misunderstandings 71–2
    overcoming stuckness 76–8

E
Edgar, James 103–7
effort versus results 165–8
exemplars 33–5

F
feedback 163–4
    see also critique
four D design process 23–6

G
glossary 184–9
grade, understanding your 165–9
    effort versus results 165–8
    student example 167–8
    subjectivity in assessment 168–9
group/peer critique 12, 13, 122, 129–30
    case study 143–5

H
Hamamoto, Chris 58–60
Hepworth, Dr Katherine 179–80

I
ideas
    creative bridges to 17–18
    defining keywords 78–80
    fear of having no new 131
    generating 78–92
    keywords and pulls to sketch 87–8
    mind maps and semiotics 88–92
    mood boards 84–6
    numbers of 71–2, 74
    visual research based on keywords 80–4
instructors, working with 122–7
    critiquing methods 122–4
    subjectivity in critique 125–7
    understanding designer talk 124–5

K
keywords 78–80
    mood boards and 84–6
    and pulls to sketch ideas 87–8
    visual research based on 80–4
Khan, Yasmin 136–8

L
learning to be creative 17–18
Leonard, Neil 103–7
loose design briefs
    case study 64–7
    versus tight design briefs 39–41
loose sketches 92–3
    case study 103–7
Lucas, Willem Henri 143–5

M
Mata, Nic 171–4
Mease, Sarah 75
mind maps 88–9, 92
mood boards 84–6

N
narrative techniques 154–60
    case study 175–8
Necon 84
North Carolina Museum of Natural Sciences (NCMNS) case study 175–8

O

'one-on-one' critique 12, 123
online
    critique 12, 13, 123–4
    presentation case study 181–3
    presentations 159–60

P

Palmer, Tony 55–7
panels see design juries
participation 130
peer/group critique 12, 13, 122, 129–30
    case study 143–5
Pop, Alison 171–4
presentations 148–60
    in appropriate format 152
    details 150–2
    explaining design problem 153
    first impressions 151
    length 148, 159
    narrative case study 175–8
    online case study 181–3
    practising 152
    preparing 151–2
    to professional and student juries 164–5
    professional style case study 171–4
    slide case study 179–80
    starting 156
    storytelling and narrative techniques 154–60
    student examples 150–2, 156–8
    talking about your work 148–50
    technological issues 152
problem spaces and problem space solutions 117–19, 127, 129
professional vision 127–9
'pulls' 80–4
    mood boards and 84–6
    to sketch ideas 87–8

Q

questions, asking 127, 129
    case study 133–5

R

Rennard, Bethany 144
results versus effort 165–8
Richards, Henry 104, 107
Ricks, Jacob 93, 94

S

semiotics 89–92
signs 89–92
sketches and drafts 92–7
    loose sketches 92–3
    loose sketches case study 103–7
    pen and computer 95–7
    tight sketches 94–5
    tight sketches case study 108–11
    using keywords and pulls 87–8
slide presentation case study 179–80
Sparacino, Alyssa 63
spellcheckers 152
storytelling 154–60
    case study 175–8
stuckness 73–5
    methods to overcome 76–8
subjectivity
    in assessment 168–9
    case study 136–8
    in critique 125–7
Sueda, Jon 99–102
'sunk cost' 116

T

talk, understanding designer 124–5
talking about your work 148–50
Tandiharja, Yovina Kristiani 57
taste, designer's 120–1, 165
Tegtmeyer, Rebecca 43–4
Thame, Matt 103–7
tight design briefs
    case study 54–7
    versus loose design briefs 39–41
tight sketches 94–5
    case study 108–11
Tran, Tracy 68

U

uncertainty, being comfortable with 119–20

W

'wicked' design problems 117
Worthington, Michael, 63 139–42
written content 42–4

Z

Zahabi, Liese 64–7
Zhai, Lemon 63

ACKNOWLEDGEMENTS

We would like to thank Louise Baird-Smith for offering us this opportunity. Her vision drove the book's structure and made us think deeply about all the things we don't say to our students in the classroom. A big thank you to our editor Leafy, who patiently worked with us across three time zones, always offering helpful perspective and advice.
A big thank you to our design teacher contributors who generously opened their practice to us and patiently responded to requests for read-thru and edits. Our families have been supportive and understanding about giving us time to write and to think.

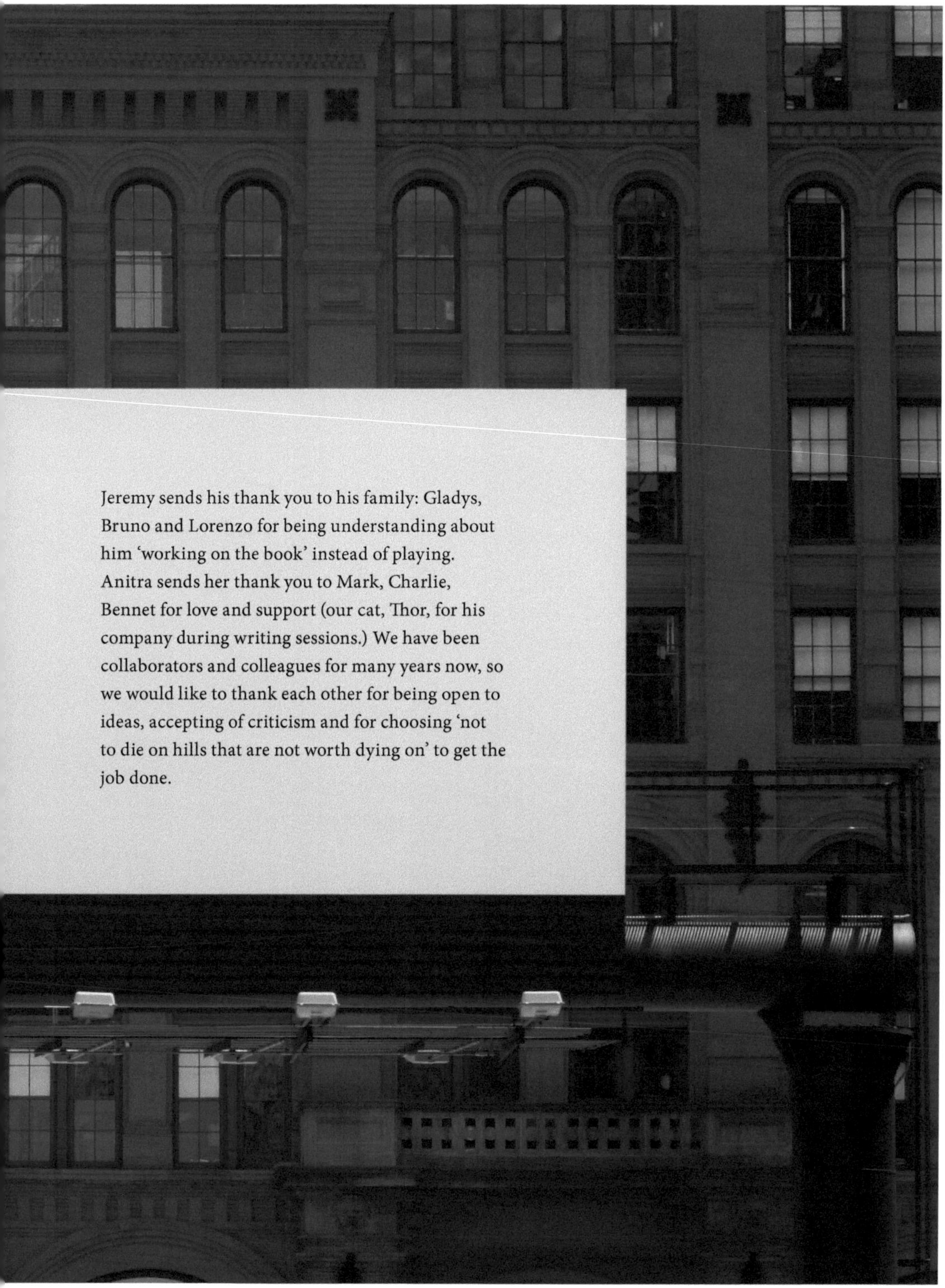

Jeremy sends his thank you to his family: Gladys, Bruno and Lorenzo for being understanding about him 'working on the book' instead of playing. Anitra sends her thank you to Mark, Charlie, Bennet for love and support (our cat, Thor, for his company during writing sessions.) We have been collaborators and colleagues for many years now, so we would like to thank each other for being open to ideas, accepting of criticism and for choosing 'not to die on hills that are not worth dying on' to get the job done.

END